Constitution and Government of India

CONSTITUTION AND GOVERNMENT OF INDIA

UTTARA SAHASRABUDDHE
Former Professor and Head
Department of Civics and Politics
University of Mumbai

PHI Learning Private Limited
Delhi-110092
2025

In fond memory of ***Shri Asoke K. Ghosh*** *(October 1942–February 2024), Founder Chairman and Managing Director of PHI Learning, whose vision endlessly inspires.*

The Legacy Continues... .

Published by Pushpita Ghosh, PHI Learning Private Limited, Rimjhim House, 111, Patparganj Industrial Estate, Delhi-110092 and Printed by Syndicate Binders, A-20, Hosiery Complex, Noida, Phase-II Extension, Noida-201305 (N.C.R. Delhi).

₹395.00

Constitution and Government of India
Uttara Sahasrabuddhe

ISBN-978-93-5443-870-7 (Print Book)
ISBN-978-93-5443-895-0 (e-Book)

Contents

Preface

A constitution is a living document. It evolves through its implementation and interpretation, as well as through amendments. As a constitution is primarily about power—of the government and the citizens—it is as much political as it is legal.

During my student days, my understanding of the Indian Constitution was shaped by two of my teachers—Mr. V.K. Sinha in the undergraduate classes and Professor Dr. Nawaz Mody in the post-graduate classes. Mr. Sinha's approach provided a rational criticism of the Constitution; while Professor Mody combined in her teaching, the 'legal' and the 'political' in quite an exciting way.

I taught the courses in Constitution, Government and Politics of India for over fifteen years to undergraduate classes. It was at this time that I began to realise the lacunae in the standard syllabi of (and hence, standard textbooks on) the Constitution of India. I always felt that the approach to teaching of the Constitution needs a re-think. While this issue was sidelined after I joined the PG Department (where I did not teach courses related to the Constitution), it did remain with me; and I continued to think over it intermittently.

Retirement from the University provided me the opportunity to finalise my ideas. Thus, I began to write a book that explains Constitutional provisions in the context of Constitutional Assembly Debates, as well as amendments and court judgements, bringing in the historical, political and evolutionary nature of Constitutional provisions. I hope the students, teachers and general readers will appreciate the book.

I welcome any constructive suggestions for the improvement of the book.

Uttara Sahasrabuddhe

Acknowledgements

At the outset, I wish to express deep sense of gratitude to my friends who were the initial readers of chapters of this book. Professor Dr. Vaibhavi Palsule read a few chapters and gave very useful suggestions towards making this book readable for students and general readers alike. Dr. Akshay Ranade, Dr. Ajinkya Gaikwad and Dr. Gayatri Lele, my young friends and colleagues with sharp intellect and critical mind, enthusiastically devoted time to read all chapters. Their involvement and interest in this book were no less than my own. Their suggestions, criticism and insights on the book, which I received through our many lengthy conversations, have helped me improve various aspects of the book. Dr. Vishakha Patil, always a very reliable colleague, has read the chapters and helped me with formulating questions and project suggestions for each chapter. My brother Indrajit Sathe, sister-in-law Dr. Madhavi Sathe, my sister Chitra Maslekar, brother-in-law Air Cmde. (Retd.) Dr. Rahul Maslekar have obliged by reading a chapter or two each, and have made valuable suggestions towards improving readability of the book. Their comments have been quite helpful; as all of them are professional in, and have expertise in, fields completely different from Political Science. Comments on one chapter by my niece Ashwini Maslekar, who is working in education sector, have been helpful and encouraging. Above all, my husband Pramod was the first reader and critic of each chapter. I extend heartfelt thanks to all of them.

I wish to thank the PHI Learning Team for their interest in this book, especially to Ms. Babita Misra for her useful editorial suggestions and the periodic nudge that helped me to complete this book.

Uttara Sahasrabuddhe

List of Abbreviations

CA—Constituent Assembly
CEC—Chief Election Commissioner
CM—Chief Minister
CJ—Chief Justice (of High Court)
CJI—Chief Justice of India
CoM—Council of Ministers
DC—Drafting Committee
DC-1948—Draft Constitution of 1948
DP/DPs—Directive Principle/s
EC—Election Commissioner
ECI—Election Commission of India
FC—Finance Commission
GoI—Government of India
GST—Goods & Services Tax
HC/s—High Court/s
NITI Ayog—National Institution for Transforming India
NJAC—National Judicial Appointments Commission
PC—Planning Commission
PIL—Public Interest Litigation
PM—Prime Minister
PMO—Prime Minister's Office
SC—Supreme Court of India

1

Making of the Constitution

It is important to understand a few terms at the outset. One of these is, a 'state'. In Political and Social Sciences, this term is used to indicate two types of legal entities. A state means a legal-political entity that has a specific territory, occupied by its citizens; that additionally has a government; and that is 'sovereign'. The term 'sovereign' indicates the power to govern own affairs as well as freedom from any external control. Thus, India is a state, by this definition; and so are the US, Russia, Pakistan, Indonesia, Myanmar, the UAE, Argentina, etc. However, the term 'state' also has another meaning—a unit of government in a federal country. Thus, Maharashtra, Tamil Nadu, Assam, Punjab, etc. are states in India. The term state is used to indicate a unit in a federation only in a few countries like the US, India, Australia. In many other countries, the term 'province' is used for the same, e.g. Canada, Pakistan. During the British period, administrative units of British India were called 'provinces'.

Another term that needs to be explained is a 'constitution' of a state. It is a written document that details the organisation of government of that state, rights of the people and corresponding limitations on the powers of the government. While most constitutions in the world today are written documents, the constitution of England is unwritten, and is based on customs, conventions and practices.

Constituent Assembly (CA) of India came into existence in 1946. This body prepared and enacted the Constitution for independent India. However, it is important to understand that the Constitution, beginning with its first draft, as well as the debates in the CA were shaped by a history of many decades prior to the formation of the CA.

The British Government had started to reform its administration in India after the War of 1857. But since the early twentieth century, they began to feel the heat of aspirational and agitational politics of a new class of Indian leaders. They responded by making laws that introduced small steps of self-government in India. The Indian demand for self-government was a product of British education. The small but vocal class of educated Indians gave voice to the agony of the colonised people and their aspiration for freedom. This class was influenced by the modern Western ideas like nationalism, freedom, self-rule, constitutionalism and representative government. With the rise of the national movement, Indians began aspiring for greater role in administration, and attaining self-government eventually.

These aspirations took the form of petitions to the British Government initially. Agitations for the demand of self-government replaced petitions, once the Extremists[1] began to dominate the national movement. This led to a series of documents produced by Indian nationalists of different hues, making concrete demands for greater and greater representation in administration and government from time to time. Most of these documents, written by Indians who had imbibed Western values through their education, reflected Western ideas predominantly, and understandably so.

The colonial laws of government reform as well as the Indian documents of demands, both contributed to the "making" of the constitution. This historical process will be reviewed in this chapter.

1.1 LANDMARKS IN THE HISTORY OF CONSTITUTION[2]

Efforts to regulate the way India was governed began in the aftermath of the War of 1857. The British Government made the Indian Councils Act in 1861, and the Charter Act in 1883. Reforms were taken a step further by the Indian Councils Act 1892.[3] Parallel to these were efforts to introduce local bodies at the level of cities and villages in India. Notable among these are the resolutions passed by Governors-General Mayo (in 1870) and Ripon (in 1882); and the Resolution of 1918.[4]

Representation of Indians in government and administration continued to be negligible even after the reforms of 1892. British policies during famine and plague during the 1890's led to growing dissatisfaction among Indians. This led to the rise of extremism and emergence of secret revolutionary societies in different parts of India. Viceroy Curzon's decision to partition the province of Bengal in 1905 contributed further to massive outrage against the British Government. To oppose the partition in particular and British policies in general, the Indian National Congress (INC) adopted the policy of *swadesi* and boycott during its session in Calcutta in 1906. Morley, the Secretary of State for India, announced in the British Parliament that a committee will be appointed to prepare a report on extending representative government in India.

He believed that such reforms could help rally the moderates and tame the rising extremism. He held meetings with Gopal Krishna Gokhale, a Moderate leader of the INC, while Gokhale was on a visit to London in 1906. Around the same time, Viceroy Minto received a delegation of the Indian Muslims in Shimla. The delegation demanded separate electorates for the Muslims. The Morley-Minto Reforms, also called as the Indian Councils Act, were announced in 1909. Besides other reforms, the Act provided for separate electorates for the Muslims.[5]

Box 1.1: Indian Councils Act, 1909 (i.e. Morley-Minto Reforms)

- Introduced Elections in India for the first time, based on very limited franchise.
- Elected members to sit in central (Imperial) and provincial legislative councils, in addition to nominated members.
- Introduction of separate electorates for the Muslims.

The All India Muslim League (hereafter, referred to as Muslim League) and Moderate leaders of the INC welcomed the Indian Councils Act, 1909. However, the separate electorates for the Muslims proved to be contentious. The rules made under the 1909 Act ended up giving more representation to the Muslims than their population. Moreover, the qualifications under the rules for being a voter were more lenient for the Muslims than for the Hindus. This led to disillusionment among the members of the INC. In 1911, the British Government announced the reversal of the partition of Bengal. This led to anger among the Muslims against the Government.

The implementation of the Morley-Minto Reforms brought elected representatives of the people in the legislative councils. Their questions and scrutiny of administration brought about some accountability in governance—however limited that might have been. On the other hand, the Government became more repressive and imposed restrictions on the freedom of the people and the press.

Nineteen elected representatives of the Imperial Legislative Council made a petition to the Viceroy in 1916. Based on the experience of the Act of 1909, these members made a case for further reforms. Around 1915, with the initiative of Bal Gangadhar Tilak, and with the realisation of the need to come together against the British, the INC and the Muslim League began talks for co-operation. Situation created by the outbreak of the First World War had also necessitated such talks. The talks between the INC and the Muslim League were fruitful and the two parties agreed on a pact. The pact was accepted by both parties at their separate sessions held in Lucknow in 1916, and hence, is known as the Lucknow Pact.[6]

Box 1.2: Lucknow Pact, 1916

- Demand for separate electorates for Muslims, with proportional representation.
- Demand for equality with other British dominions.
- Demand to prevent the ICS officers from holding political office in government.
- Demand for provincial autonomy, greater power to provincial legislative council vis-à-vis the executive.

Before his death in 1915, Gokhale had prepared a proposal on reforms in government and had sent it to the Viceroy. This proposal was published in 1917. He had proposed wide reforms, like autonomy to provinces, right of the members of the legislative councils to debate the budget, etc. The extent of measures suggested by Gokhale was a kind of acceptance that further reforms following up on the 1909 Act had become necessary.

As the First World War began in 1914, many Indians joined British armed forces and fought the war along with the British forces. The number of Indians in the British Indian Army exceeded 10 lakhs. They fought on fronts in Egypt, Gallipoli, East Africa, Mesopotamia, etc. INC leaders like Tilak had proposed to co-operate with the British war efforts, thereby hoping to move further towards self-rule eventually. Indian Nationalists expected the British Government to introduce self-rule in India as an acknowledgement of the contribution of the Indians to the War. It was said that the Allied Powers were fighting for freedom and nationalism. Russia faced a revolution in the middle of the War which was welcomed across Europe and America. The then Secretary of State for India was of the opinion that these events during the War have definitely impacted the Indians; and that the British Government will have to make more fundamental changes in the Indian administration.

Edwin Montague visited India in 1917, soon after taking over as the Secretary of State for India. He met the Viceroy Chelmsford as well as representatives of various communities and interest groups. He prepared a report that evaluated the reforms introduced under previous Act; proposed to introduce limited self-government in India and to protect the interests of the minorities. The report, known as "Montford Reforms", was presented to the British Parliament in 1918. INC session held in the same year discussed the report. In a rare display of unity between the moderates and the extremists, the INC made following demands: extend autonomy also to central government; acknowledge the freedoms of expression, assembly and press; and establish equality before law. Based on the Montford report, the British Parliament passed the Government of India Act, 1919.[7] The Act introduced Dyarchy at the level of provincial government. Dyarchy means a government where power is vested in two authorities. Thus, the Act of 1919 divided the power in the provincial governments between elected representatives and the Governor.

Box 1.3: Government of India Act, 1919

- Introduced Dyarchy at the level of Provincial Governments: some portfolios were handed over to elected Indian legislators while remaining were controlled by the Governor.
- Powers of the Central and Provincial Governments were divided, creating Central list and Provincial list.
- Provided for a review of the Act after ten years.

Even before the first election was held under the Act of 1919, the British Government in India passed the Rowlatt Act in 1919. It gave the Government the power to detain anyone without any reason. M.K. Gandhi called for a nation-wide boycott against this Act. This led to the tragic incident known as Jallianwala Bagh massacre in April 1919.

There were differences within the Indian leadership in general and within the INC in particular, on whether to accept or reject the reforms under the Act of 1919. The INC ultimately boycotted the elections held in 1920. However, moderate leaders from the INC contested elections and so did the non-Brahmin party in Madras, and many Muslim leaders. Leaders like C.R. Das and Motilal Nehru left the INC to form Swaraj Party when INC continued its boycott also during the next election in 1923.

The elected representatives began to voice criticism of the Government as well as make suggestions for better governance from inside the legislative councils. But the problems with the reforms (e.g. Dyarchy) and its shortcomings (e.g. absence of power to elected members in the centre) became clearer as the elected legislatures began to function. In 1924, with M.A. Jinnah as its president, the Muslim League made a demand for a federation with full autonomy to provinces. Swaraj Party made a demand for reconsideration of the Act of 1919. A committee under the chairmanship of Home Secretary of Government of India, Alexander Muddiman, was appointed in 1924, to review the implementation of reforms under the Act of 1919. The nine-member committee submitted two reports, majority report and minority report. The majority report did not recommend any major change from the Act of 1919. However, the minority report of the Muddiman Committee concluded that the system of Dyarchy had failed and therefore, it proposed a responsible government in the provinces. When the reports came for discussion in the central legislative assembly, Motilal Nehru suggested an amendment to it. This amendment was not passed. But some of the ideas in it were later included in the Nehru Committee Report.[8]

The Government of India Act, 1919 had provided for a review of its provisions after ten years. But the Act was becoming increasingly unpopular. The British Government, thus, announced the formation of a commission to review the Act in November 1927, two years earlier than required. The seven-member Commission was headed by John Simon and came to be known as

Simon Commission. However, no single Indian was appointed on the Simon Commission as a member. This resulted in bringing the leaders of different communities and parties together in the call to boycott the Commission. Viceroy Irwin announced that whether or not Indians co-operate, the Commission will do its job and submit the report. The Simon Commission arrived in Bombay in February 1928. In the same month, INC took lead to call an all-party conference to appoint a committee to prepare an Indian draft of a constitution. A committee was appointed in May 1928 in the subsequent all-party conference. Motilal Nehru was to be the chairman of the nine-member committee. The Committee prepared its report in three months.[9] It was the first draft of a constitution prepared by Indian leaders.

Box 1.4: Nehru Committee Report, 1928

- Drafted like a Constitution.
- Claimed dominion status for India.
- Introduced parliamentary system and adult suffrage.
- Introduced Fundamental Rights of the Citizens, which included some socio-economic rights (such as elementary education, secured wages, etc.), and also the right to bear arms.
- Specifically mentioned that there will be no State Religion.
- Abolished separate electorates—introduced reservation for Muslims in the legislature, from the constituencies where they formed a minority.
- Proposed reorganisation of provinces on the basis of language.

Though the Nehru Committee was appointed by an all-party conference, parties other than INC did not willingly accept its report. Muslim League opposed the Nehru Committee Report during and since the all-party conference of 1928. In the 1929 session of Muslim League, Jinnah made various demands for the Muslims.[10] He demanded a federal government with residual powers given to the provinces; at least one-third representation in central legislature for the Muslims; separation of Sindh from Bombay province; and protection of majority status of Muslims in Punjab and Bengal in case of reorganisation of provinces.

Boycott of Simon Commission also led to the revival of agitational politics and revolutionary movement in India. Revolutionary groups resurfaced and regrouped in Bengal and other parts of the country. In its Lahore session in 1929, chaired by Jawaharlal Nehru, INC made a major shift. It shifted away from the demand of dominion status for India, and adopted a resolution demanding *Purna Swaraj*—complete independence. The Simon Commission Report was published in May 1930 in the background of these events.[11] It proposed discarding Dyarchy, introduction of responsible government in the provinces, extension of franchise, reserved constituencies for Depressed Classes, and so on.

However, the boycott by Indians on the Simon Commission rendered the exercise almost futile. Viceroy Irwin stepped in at this stage to salvage the reform process. He proposed to invite leaders of Indian political parties and representatives of Princely States to have discussion with the members of British Parliament on a possible solution to the constitutional and communal problem in India. Two such Round Table Conferences were held in London—first between November 1930 and January 1931, and the second between September and December 1931. The INC did not participate in the first Round Table Conference. But following the signing of Gandhi-Irwin Pact, INC participated in the second Round Table Conference and was represented by M.K. Gandhi.

The INC session in March 1931 in Karachi passed a resolution that came to be known as the Karachi Resolution.[12] Besides a statement on fundamental rights, the Karachi Resolution included the statement of INC's idea of socio-economic reforms in independent India.

Box 1.5: Karachi Resolution, 1931

- Included seven fundamental rights (including the right to bear arms)
- Included many socio-economic rights such as—
  - Abolition of serfdom, abolition of child labour
  - Ensuring minimum wages, right to form labour unions
- Included Social agenda—
  - Protection of women workers
  - Prohibition of intoxicating drinks and drugs
- Included Economic agenda—
  - State control of key industries and mineral resources
  - Exempting uneconomic land holdings from rent

The dual task of the Round Table Conferences was to prepare the constitution of India and to find solution to the communal problem. On the second question, Muslim leaders were firm on separate electorates and one-third membership in the central legislature. B.R. Ambedkar put forward a demand for separate electorates for the Depressed Classes. The Round Table Conferences were inconclusive. On 16 August 1932, British Prime Minister Ramsay MacDonald announced the "Communal Award".[13] Muslims, Europeans, Christians, Sikhs, Anglo-Indians and Depressed Classes secured separate communal constituencies as per the Award. Muslim League welcomed the Award, while the INC opposed it. Gandhi opposed separate electorates to the Depressed Classes and began a fast unto death against the provision. Madan Mohan Malaviya took lead in bringing together Ambedkar and Gandhi to discuss the issue. The meeting of the two leaders led to the signing of Poona Pact.[14]

Box 1.6: Poona Pact, 1932

- Opposed the provision of separate electorates for the Depressed Classes included in the Communal Award announced by the British Prime Minister; and discarded it.
- Instead, introduced the system of Joint Electorates with Reserved Seats for the Depressed Classes.

The British Government published a White Paper on constitutional reforms in India in 1933 and the same was referred to the joint committee of the British Parliament. The joint committee gave its report in October 1934. Subsequently a bill was introduced in the British Parliament in December 1934 and was passed in August 1935. This came to be known as the Government of India Act, 1935.[15] The Act contained eleven parts and ten schedules; and was the most extensive government and administrative reform made by the British Government in India.

Box 1.7: Government of India Act, 1935

- Created 'Federation of India' with two levels of government—the Central Government; and below it the governments in the Provinces and the Princely States.
- Abolished Dyarchy at the Provincial level, introduced elected provincial legislatures.
- Franchise expanded—from earlier 3% of population to include 14% of population.
- Dyarchy introduced at the Central level—but subjects like defence, foreign affairs were retained under the direct control of the Governor-General.
- Governors of Provinces entrusted with emergency powers.
- Proposed establishment of Federal Court and the Reserve Bank of India.
- Introduced separate electorates for the Sikhs, in addition to those for Muslims—but no separate electorates for Depressed Classes.

Both INC and Muslim League expressed their dissatisfaction over the Act of 1935. Nonetheless, both decided to contest the elections held under the Act. The elections were conducted in 1936–37. The INC won maximum number of seats if the number in all eleven provinces is put together. It could form governments in six provinces. On the other hand, the Muslim League did not win majority of Muslim seats. Most Muslim seats were won by regional Muslim parties/organisations.

In its 1937 session, the Muslim League for the first time adopted a resolution demanding the creation of a separate state of Pakistan. Since then, it pursued this goal in various ways.

Leaders of various Indian political parties like Hindu Mahasabha (V.D. Savarkar), Liberal Party (Chimanlal Setalvad, and Cowasji Jehangir), Lokshahi Swaraj Party (N.C. Kelkar and Jamnadas Mehta) and leader of Depressed

Classes B.R. Ambedkar, together sent a joint petition to the Viceroy on 3 October 1939. The petition argued that it would be wrong to assume that the INC and Muslim League were the only representatives of the Indian people. The petition further said that to assume that INC is the only party in the country would amount to destroying democracy.[16] The diversity that this petition talked about was reflected in the reactions of various Indian political parties to the Second World War that began in 1939.

The Congress Working Committee resolved that if Britain and its allies are fighting the War to protect freedom and democracy, then British Government must clarify how these objectives apply to India; and that the INC would not support Britain's war until then. INC later asked its provincial governments to resign. Muslim League offered conditional support to the War. Hindu Mahasabha extended support to the War and Savarkar urged the Hindu youth to join the British armed forces in large number. The Liberal Party extended unconditional support to the War and so did the Radical Democratic Party of M.N. Roy. The Indian Communist Party criticised the War initially. But supported the War after Hitler's Germany attacked Soviet Union. Such was the diversity referred to by the petition of party leaders mentioned above.

Indeed, the CA too mirrored this diversity, as will be seen below. The diversity is manifest in the lengthy and intense debates during the constitution making process, as will be seen in subsequent chapters.

Early in 1942, the Japanese forces attacked Burma and occupied Rangoon. The advance of Japanese forces posed direct threat to British India, particularly the Assam province. In addition to this, pressure from US President Roosevelt and his own coalition partner in the War Cabinet, the Labour Party, led the British Prime Minister Churchill to send Stafford Cripps to India to negotiate with Indian leaders. Cripps arrived in India in March 1942 and immediately announced his plan.[17] The Cripps Plan declared that India would have the freedom to withdraw from the Commonwealth of Nations. It further said that a constituent assembly for India will be formed as soon as the War will be over. This assembly will be elected indirectly by the members of the provincial legislatures. The Cripps Plan assured that the British Government will implement the constitution created by the constituent assembly. It provided that until a new constitution comes into existence, defence of British India will remain a responsibility of the British Government.

Cripps met several Indian leaders of different political parties during March-April 1942. However, most Indian parties rejected the Cripps Plan for various reasons. One provision in the Cripps Plan became a major cause of its failure. The Plan had provided that in case one or many provinces do not wish to participate in making a constitution for the entire country, such province/s will be allowed to make their own constitution. Further, such provinces will have the same status as that of the independent Indian State. It practically meant that such States could separate from India and form another independent State. Similar power was given to the princely states too in the Cripps Plan. This provision clearly was made to pave way for a partition of India. It is no surprise that it was rejected by the INC.

Box 1.8: Points to Remember

- While the origins of administrative reforms in India go back to the late nineteenth century, self-rule began to take shape, step by step, only in the twentieth century.
- Each reform was made to tame the anger of the Indians against the British. Each Act of reform was a step ahead in the direction of self-rule. However, every such Act fell short of expectations and aspirations of Indians at that point of time.
- Despite dissatisfaction, many Indians sought entry in the provincial and central legislatures through these reforms. This was perceived as an instrument of bringing about change from within the system, though it was only partly successful.
- The demand of the Muslims for separate representation was an important determining factor in the process of reforms.

1.2 THE CONSTITUENT ASSEMBLY

War in Europe came to an end with the surrender of Germany in May 1945. The newly elected Government of Clement Attlee decided to send a committee to India with the objective to resolve the question of future of India. The committee consisting of Pethic-Lawrence, Stafford Cripps and A.V. Alexander declared a plan on16 May 1946, which is known as the Cabinet Mission plan. The Plan suggested the creation of a constituent assembly. And dividing provinces in groups with these groups having their own legislature and executive—in addition to the provincial legislatures and executives.[18] Both INC and Muslim League accepted the Plan, though each had expressed some reservations about it. Subsequently in 1946, elections to provincial legislatures were held and the newly elected legislatures, in turn, elected the members of the Constituent Assembly (CA) of India.

As per the Cabinet Mission Plan, an Interim Government was appointed by the Viceroy to expedite the process of transfer of power. The Muslim League did not join the Interim Government initially, but changed its decision later and joined. Nehru was appointed the Vice President of Viceroy's Executive Council—*de facto* Prime Minister of the Interim Government.[19]

The first meeting of the CA was convened on 9 December 1946. However, Jinnah had given a call to the Muslim League members to boycott the CA. Thus, "a fourth of the nation was not represented at the Assembly's deliberations".[20]

On 20 February 1947, the British Government announced that it will withdraw from India by the end of June 1948. However, Viceroy Mountbatten convinced the British Government that the British withdrawal should be completed earlier. Thus, he announced on 3 June 1947 that Britain would leave India on 15 August and that it would recognize the existence of two independent states on the sub-continent, India and Pakistan.[21] Thus, colonial rule ended with the partition of British India.

The composition of the CA changed due to partition. It originally comprised 389 members, but was left with 299 members after partition.

TABLE 1.1 Composition of the Constituent Assembly

Members from	*Number/Number post-partition*	*Mode*
Provinces	292/229	Elected by Provincial Assemblies by a single transferable vote
Princely States	93/70	Nominated
Chief Commissioner's Provinces	04/0	—
Total	389/299	

The diversity of the political class of India mentioned earlier in this chapter was also reflected in the CA. While an overwhelming majority of the members of the CA came from INC, people from other political parties were elected too. Members representing Liberal Party, Hindu Mahasabha, Scheduled Caste Federation, etc. were on the CA. Many persons elected on the INC ticket were not members of the party. The party went out of the way to get them elected in order to ensure that best talent becomes the part of the drafting process.[22] Ideological diversity was reflected even within the members of the INC, some tending to be more socialist, some more conservative and so on.[23]

Box 1.9: Post-Partition Constituent Assembly

- Total 299 Members—nearly 80% elected on Congress ticket—other parties represented included, Hindu Mahasabha, Scheduled Caste Federation, Akali Dal, Anglo-Indian Association, Muslim League, Socialist Party, National Conference, CPI.
- Included members from all religious communities—included 15 women
- Represented wide ideological diversity within and between parties.
- Had formed four committees: Committee on Rules & Procedures; Advisory Committee on Fundamental Rights, Minorities and Tribal and Excluded Areas; Provincial Constitution Committee; Committee on Chief Commissioner's Provinces.
- Had formed five sub-committees: on Fundamental Rights; on Minorities; on the North East Frontier (Assam) Tribal and Excluded Areas; and Sub-Committees I and II appointed by the Provincial Constitution Committee.
- Out of 299, only 58 members were appointed on the nine committees and sub-committees—among these 58, 28 were members of one committee; 19 were members of two committees; 5 members were on three committees each; 5 members were on four committees each; and 1 member was on five committees.

(Contd.)

Box 1.9: Post-Partition Constituent Assembly

- First session was held on 9 December 1946—first post-partition session was held on 31 December 1947.
- Completed the task of writing the constitution in 166 days, 11 sessions, spread over 2 years 11 months.

"Alternative" Visions

By mid-1940's, many people in India had begun to sense that formation of a constituent assembly could take place in near future. Thus, thinking over a constitution of free India had begun. Different parties and interests wanted to put forward their ideas and wished to influence the future constitution.

One such document produced was the "Constitution of the Hindusthan Free State". Hindu Mahasabha entrusted the task of preparing a draft constitution to Bhopatkar Satkar Nidhi, a group in Poona. A committee, consisting of members like N.C. Kelkar, L.B. Bhopatkar, etc. and chaired by D.V. Gokhale, was appointed for the purpose.[24] Many provisions in the draft are similar to the final constitution; as both were inspired by Western ideals, and both sought to maintain a continuity with the Government of India Act, 1935. Despite being drafted by Hindu Mahasabha, this document recommended equal rights for all, including the freedom of religion; and it specified no state religion for Hindusthan. There was, however, one innovative recommendation in the draft that was never seriously considered by the CA—the inclusion of instruments of direct democracy, like referendum, initiative and recall.[25] S.P. Mookerjee, former President of Hindu Mahasabha, was a member of the Interim Government and also of the CA. During the debates in the CA, "Mookerjee raised those principles from the Constitution of the Hindusthan Free State that were broadly aligned with the majority of the members of the Constituent Assembly".[26]

Box 1.10: Constitution of the Hindusthan Free State, 1944

- Proposed a Federation of Hindusthan, which would be democratic and republican and have equal rights for all.
- Specifically expressed that there will be no State Religion.
- Perceived rights to liberty and property as inherent and proposed them as inviolable rights.
- Included Fundamental Rights such as Equality, right to bear arms, freedom not to attend religious education in public schools.
- Included the rights to free elementary education, secured living wages, welfare of children etc., as Fundamental Rights.
- Proposed devices of direct democracy for people, such as Initiative, Referendum and Recall, both at federal and provincial levels.

Another draft of a constitution was written by M.N. Roy, leader of the Radical Democratic Party. It was named "Constitution of Free India".[27] The draft was based on radical Marxist ideas. While some of the socio-economic rights included in the draft were reflected in the draft of the Indian Constitution and indeed, some became a part of the Constitution; most of its radical ideas did not have any bearing upon the debates in the CA.

Box 1.11: Constitution of Free India, 1944

Proposed an alternate vision of free India—had many features similar to the then existing Communist States, such as:

- People's Committees with sweeping powers including rights to recall, initiate legislation, etc.
- Inclusion of many economic and social rights as Fundamental Rights.
- State ownership of resources such as land, industry, etc.

Gandhian concept of government was an important alternate vision to the Western vision of a democratic constitution. It preferred village-led government over centralised government; and fundamental duties over fundamental rights. In 1938, Gandhi himself was involved in writing the Constitution for a Princely State of Aundh (in present day Maharashtra), at the request of the Raja of the State. The team included Appa Pant (the son of the Raja of Aundh) and Maurice Frydman, an aide to Gandhi. The Constitution made village panchayats the base of democracy; and was promulgated in Aundh State in 1939.[28] Another effort to write a Constitution based on Gandhian principles was undertaken by S.N. Agarwal. He prepared a draft constitution called "Gandhian Constitution for Free India".[29] Gandhi himself wrote a foreword to it. While the members of the CA created a Constitution based primarily on the Western idea of democracy; the idea of strengthening village panchayats found its way in the Constitution in the form of a Directive Principle.[30]

Box 1.12: Gandhian Constitution, 1946

- Proposed a decentralised polity based on village panchayats.
- Proposed not only Fundamental Rights, but also Fundamental Duties of the Citizens—such as duty to promote public welfare by contributing to State funds, avoid and resist exploitation of man by man.

As early as in 1930, B.R. Ambedkar, along with R. Srinivasan, prepared a memorandum for the protection of the Depressed Classes in the future constitution of India.[31] In 1945, while addressing the Annual Session of the All India Scheduled Caste Federation, Ambedkar gave a scheme to resolve the question of proper representation to various communities.[32] As a member of the Sub-Committee on fundamental Rights, Ambedkar submitted the States and Minorities Report to the Sub-Committee, on behalf of the Scheduled Caste Federation.[33]

Box 1.13: States and Minorities Report, 1947

- Designated the independent country as "the United States of India".
- Treated Fundamental Rights as inviolable and gave a detailed list of protections against violation of Rights.
- Under the title "Protection against Economic Exploitation", the Report suggested nationalisation of key industry and agriculture.
- Made provisions for the protection of minorities as well as the Scheduled Castes—ensuring representation in Executive, Legislature and Services; providing for education of Scheduled Castes.

Writing of the Constitution

The CA began to function in December 1946 and worked for nearly three years to complete the task of writing the constitution of independent India. The following table explains the various stages in the process.

TABLE 1.2 Stages of Constitution-Making[34]

Stage	*Dates*	*Business*
First Session	9 December 1946–22 January 1947	Introduction of the Objectives Resolution by Jawaharlal Nehru–adoption of the same by CA
Second Session–Committee Stages	27 February 1947–30 August 1947	Several Committees (as mentioned in Box 1.9) were formed to examine and report on various aspects of the constitution
Preparation of Draft	1 February 1947–31 October 1947	B.N. Rau, the Constitutional Advisor, prepared a draft constitution based on the reports of the committees and debates in the CA thereupon
Drafting Committee	27 October 1947–21 February 1948	Drafting Committee examined the draft of Rau, other notes and memoranda; made changes and prepared the final draft
Public Circulation of the Draft	21 February 1948–26 October 1948	Public circulation of the draft–comments and suggestions were received and scrutinised by relevant Committees–Drafting Committee compiled a new version of the draft
Debates on Draft Constitution	4 November 1948	Debates on the Draft Constitution in the CA
Second Reading of Draft Constitution	15 November 1948–17 October 1949	Clause-by-clause discussion of each Article of the Draft Constitution in the CA

(Contd.)

Stage	*Dates*	*Business*
Revision of Draft Constitution	Completed on 14 November 1949	Drafting Committee revised the Draft Constitution based on the debates during first and second reading of the Draft
Third Reading of Draft Constitution	14 November 1949–26 November 1949	Few debates–members expressed satisfaction at the final Draft–motion to adopt the Constitution passed on 26 November 1949
Enactment and Adoption	26 January 1950	Constitution came into effect

Making of the constitution was, thus, a task meticulously executed. The records of the CA debates are a testimony to it. One realises the length, depth and intensity of the exercise while reading CA debates. Each subsequent chapter in this book will refer to the CA debates to understand the background of the constitutional provisions and their evolution. It may also be noted here, however, that while the provisions of the DC-1948 were vigorously debated in CA, much of the criticism of the draft provisions and suggestions thereon failed to translate into changes in the draft. Most amendments to the provisions of the DC-1948 that were adopted came from the members of the Drafting Committee (DC) including its chairperson. Many amendments suggested by other members of the CA were defeated by majority.

The Constitution thus created, has encountered criticism too. One important criticism that was made during the period of its making, and continues to be made even today, is that it has nothing new, and it is a mere copy of provisions of other constitutions and particularly of the Government of India Act, 1935. Arghya Sengupta argues that despite the fact that the Government of India Act, 1935 was roundly criticised by the Indian leadership, there is a remarkable similarity between the Act and the Indian Constitution. While accepting the need for "preference for familiarity in a fluid and fast-changing political atmosphere"; Sengupta regrets the fact that India, thus, inherited colonial institutions "designed to rule from above".[35]

However, Ambedkar had explained the position of the DC on this in quite explicit words in his speech while presenting the DC-1948 to the CA. Replying to criticism of 'copy' and 'plagiarism', Ambedkar argued, "The only new things, if there can be any, in a Constitution framed so late in the day are the variations made to remove the faults and to accommodate it to the needs of the country."[36] Regarding the similarities between the Government of India Act, 1935 and the DC-1948, Ambedkar clearly said, "I make no apologies" for it. He went on to explain that the sections replicated from the Act of 1935 relate mostly to the details of administration. While such details could have been left to the legislature for drafting, it would be unwise to do so in a country which does not have a democratic culture.[37] The criticism that the Indian Constitution is a patch-work created out of various provisions from different constitutions may indeed be valid. However, it is important to understand the circumstances—both contemporary and historical—within which the constitution was being drafted. Ambedkar's remarks help understand those circumstances.

1.3 PREAMBLE OF THE CONSTITUTION

During the first session of the CA, on 13 December 1946, Jawaharlal Nehru introduced the Objectives Resolution. While moving the resolution, Nehru said, it "seeks to show how we shall lead India to gain the objectives led down in it." He continued, "It is an undertaking with ourselves and the millions of our brothers and sisters who live in this great country. ... it will be a sort of pledge that we shall have to carry out."[38] After a lengthy discussion, the resolution was adopted on 22 January 1947. The language and spirit of the Objectives Resolution influenced greatly the Preamble of the Indian Constitution. Moreover, the Preamble also draws influence from the Karachi Resolution, 1931 (discussed above).

The Preamble was included in the DC-1948 and tabled for debate in the CA on 21 February 1948; and was adopted by the CA later.

Box 1.14: PREAMBLE

WE, THE PEOPLE OF INDIA, having solemnly resolved to constitute India into a SOVEREIGN *SOCIALIST SECULAR* DEMOCRATIC REPUBLIC and to secure to all its citizens:

JUSTICE, social, economic and political;

LIBERTY of thought, expression, belief, faith and worship;

EQUALITY of status and of opportunity;

and to promote among them all

FRATERNITY assuring the dignity of the individual and the unity and integrity of the Nation;

IN OUR CONSTITUENT ASSEMBLY this twenty-sixth day of November, 1949, do HEREBY ADOPT, ENACT AND GIVE TO OURSELVES THIS CONSTITUTION.

(**Note:** Words in *italics* were inserted by the Forty Second Amendment, 1976.)

The Preamble of a written constitution is a window to the ethos and philosophy of that constitution. It seeks to lay down the objectives that the constitution seeks to achieve. Even if it is not an "enforceable" part of the Constitution, the Preamble of the Indian Constitution helps understand the basic philosophy of the Constitution. Moreover, the Courts in India have referred to the ideals in the Preamble as a source of interpretation of law.[39] Each word or phrase in capital letters is significant because it indicates a guiding value or a fundamental principle.

TABLE 1.3 Significance of the Terms in the Preamble

Term	*Significance*
WE THE PEOPLE OF INDIA	The CA was elected under a British law and by indirect election. By use of this phrase, the Preamble, however, locates the source of authority in the People of India.
SOVEREIGN	Hence, it proclaims India as a country free from any external control and in firm control of its own destiny, i.e., Sovereign;
SOCIALIST	Aiming to achieve a "Welfare State", assuming an active role of the State in bringing social reform and economic equality;
SECULAR	Guaranteeing equal treatment of all religions and equal rights to people of all faiths;
DEMOCRATIC	Having a representative and responsible Government based on Adult Suffrage–the institutions of which are described in detail in the Constitution;
REPUBLIC	Having an elected Head of the State–thus, ending the authority of the British Crown over India.
JUSTICE	It vows to secure social justice in a society organised hierarchically; economic justice amidst disparities; and thereby create conditions for meaningful political participation for all citizens. The Directive Principles in the Constitution show the way to ensuring justice.
LIBERTY	It vows to secure basic rights of all and protect the freedom of all individuals. Fundamental Rights in the Constitution guarantee these freedoms.
EQUALITY	It vows to eliminate discrimination to secure equal status of all citizens and provide equal opportunity to all. Fundamental Rights and Directive Principles together pave way towards equality.
FRATERNITY	It aims to attain national unity and integration in the society of individuals having equal rights and status.
ADOPT, ENACT AND GIVE TO OURSELVES THIS CONSTITUTION	Having located the source of authority in the People of India, the Preamble announces on behalf of the People the adoption and enactment of the Constitution; thus, reiterating that the People themselves are the source of authority and have exercised that authority.

A batch of petitions were filed in the Supreme Court in 2020, challenging the insertion of words "socialist" and "secular" in the Constitution by Forty Second Amendment, 1976. The SC dismissed these pleas as not worth a detailed adjudication. The bench of CJI Sanjiv Khanna and Justice Sanjay Kumar said in their order, "The word 'secular' denotes a Republic that upholds equal respect for all religions. 'Socialist' represents a Republic dedicated to eliminating all forms of exploitation—whether social, political, or economic".[40] The judges clarified further that socialism in the Indian context means the commitment to function as a Welfare State.

It may be worth mentioning here, that a well-known British political scientist Ernest Barker included the Preamble of the Indian Constitution as a prologue to one of his books. He said in his preface to the book, "I am proud that the people of India should begin their independent life by subscribing to the principles of a political tradition which we in the West call Western, but which is now something more than Western."[41]

1.4 THE NEED FOR AND THE PROCESS OF AMENDING THE CONSTITUTION

Any political system along with all its elements is constantly evolving. It is imperative, therefore, that a constitution, that forms the foundation and a regulatory force of a democratic political system, also changes with time. A constitution must be a "living document" in that sense. Constitutions do change through use and implementation. They also change due to interpretation and reinterpretation of its provisions by the judiciary. This is the informal way of changing the constitution. On the other hand, constitutions can be changed by a formal procedure called amendment. In most democratic countries, the authority to make formal amendments to the constitution is vested in the legislature.

However, most experts, while acknowledging the need for change, also caution against reckless change. For example, Rajeev Bhargava argues, "We cannot treat the Constitution with sanctimonious reverence, too sacred to be touched, nor can we allow frivolous attempts to revise the Constitution every time a political deadlock occurs or there is a new government in power."[42]

Members of the CA were predominantly in favour of including a formal amending procedure in the constitution. The dispute was on how rigid or flexible the procedure should be. Members like A.K. Ayyar, K.M. Munshi, K.T. Shah, S.P. Mookerjee were in favour of amending the constitution by 2/3 majority in the Parliament *and* ratification by provincial legislatures. On the other hand, Jawaharlal Nehru, P.S Deshmukh and H.V. Kamath were in favour of a much simpler amending procedure.[43]

Ambedkar's speech on 4 November 1948 in the CA while tabling the Draft Constitution of 1948 (DC-1948) for debate, throws light on the way he was thinking about the amending procedure.[44] He started by arguing that the

DC-1948 is federal because it creates a dual polity. But it is different from the American federal constitution. First, he says, the states in US have separate constitutions, but there will be no such thing in India. Secondly, Ambedkar argued, federalism suffers from two weaknesses, rigidity and legalism. A federal constitution must necessarily be written and rigid. However, the DC-1948 provides one mean to avoid this rigidity inherent in a federation. It provides for an amending procedure whereby "very large part of the Constitution can be amended by Parliament by a double majority, namely, a majority of not less than two thirds of the members of each House present and voting and by a majority of the total membership of each House. The amendment of these Articles does not require ratification by the States."[45] A second method of amendment that he suggested required 2/3 majority in parliament plus ratification by 1/2 state legislatures.[46]

Article 304 of the DC-1948 which stipulated the amending procedures came up for debate in the CA on 17 September 1949. P.S. Deshmukh and H.V. Kamath moved amendment in favour of amendment by simple majority in parliament to the Article.[47] Both amendments were negated after a debate.

Final version of the Constitution provides for Article 368 in Part XX, titled "Power of Parliament to Amend the Constitution and the Procedure Therefor", which stipulates the procedure to amend the Constitution. It primarily prescribes two procedures.

TABLE 1.4 Amending Procedure

Provisions in the Constitution	*Procedure to Amend*
(a) article 54, article 55, article 73, article 162, article 241 or article 279A; or (b) Chapter IV of Part V, Chapter V of Part VI, or Chapter I of Part XI; or (c) any of the Lists in the Seventh Schedule; or (d) the representation of States in Parliament; or (e) the provisions of this article	2/3 majority in each House of Parliament which is not less than ½ of its total membership; and ratification by ½ of State Legislatures
Most Other Provisions	2/3 majority in each House of Parliament which is not less than ½ of its total membership

Further, "By providing that the alteration of certain provisions of the Constitution were *'not to be deemed to be amendment of the Constitution'* .... such provisions can be altered by the Union Parliament .... by a simple majority."[48]

The amending procedure and amendability of the Constitution have been subject of litigation as well as amendment several times. These will be discussed in the subsequent chapters, particularly with reference to the Fundamental Rights.

QUESTIONS

Write Short Answers (5 marks each):

1. What were the reforms introduced by the Indian Councils Act, 1909?
2. What were the reforms introduced by the Government of India Act, 1919?
3. Bring out the significance of the Nehru Committee Report, 1928.
4. Write a note on the Karachi Resolution, 1931.
5. Why was the Poona Pact signed in 1932 and how did it affect the political representation of the Depressed Classes?
6. List the key proposals of the Cabinet Mission Plan (1946), and the reasons why both the INC and Muslim League accept it despite reservations.
7. What are the risks in making a constitution either too rigid or too flexible?
8. Explain the process of amending the Constitution.

Answer the Following (15 Marks each):

1. Explain the provisions of the Government of India Act, 1935. Why was it called the most comprehensive reform?
2. "The British introduced administrative reforms in India, but each reform fell short of Indian aspirations." Discuss whether this was a deliberate strategy to retain control, or a failure to understand Indian demands?
3. "The Preamble reflects the philosophy and core principles of the Indian Constitution." Comment.

PROJECT SUGGESTIONS

1. Create a timeline highlighting the key events in the making of the Indian Constitution from 1946 to 1950.
2. Design a comic strip or infographic showcasing important milestones in the making of the Indian Constitution.
3. Prepare a PPT on the various Committees and Sub-Committees of the Constituent Assembly, depicting the members, the work assigned to the Committee/Sub-Committee.
4. Prepare a PPT that brings out the common elements and differences from the "alternate" constitutional drafts.

ENDNOTES

1. The Indian National Congress was divided into two factions—the Moderates who preferred constitutional means of making demands to the British Government, such as petitions; and the Extremists, who resorted to agitational means for the same.
2. Details of history in this section are based on Govind Talwalkar *Sattantar* (in Marathi), Volume 1 (Mauj Prakashan Gruha, 1983).
3. R. Coupland, The Constitutional Problem of India, (Oxford University Press, 1944); accessed at Constitutional Problem In India : Coupland, R. : Free Download, Borrow, and Streaming : Internet Archive.
4. For details, see Aditi Shekhawat and Ritesh Dhyani "Evolution of Local Self-Government in British India", *Indian Journal of Law and Legal Research*, Vol IV, Issue V.
5. For details, see Indian Councils Act, 1909 Archives - Constitution of India.
6. For details, see The Congress-League Scheme 1916 (INC & AIML) Archives - Constitution of India.
7. For details, see Government of India Act, 1919 Archives - Constitution of India.
8. The amendment suggested by Motilal Nehru is quoted in Talwalkar, *op cit*, p 116.
9. For details, see Nehru Report (Motilal Nehru,1928) Archives - Constitution of India.
10. Talwalkar, *op cit*, p 127.
11. Talwalkar, *op cit*, pp 139–140.
12. Karachi Resolution 1931 (Indian National Congress) Archives - Constitution of India.
13. Talwalkar, *op cit*, pp 159.
14. For details, see Poona Pact 1932 (B.R Ambedkar and M.K Gandhi) Archives - Constitution of India.
15. For details, see Government of India Act 1935 Archives - Constitution of India.
16. Talwalkar, *op cit*, p 187.
17. Talwalkar, *op cit*, p 232.
18. For details, see Cabinet Mission Plan (Cabinet Mission, 1946) Archives - Constitution of India.
19. Granville Austin, The Indian Constitution: Cornerstone of a Nation, (Clarendon Press, 1966), pp 6.

20. *Ibid* p 7.
21. *Ibid* p 8.
22. Arghya Sengupta, *The Colonial Constitution,* (Juggernaught, 2023), p 21.
23. Austin explains the diversity and also the efforts taken by the INC in ensuring it. See Austin *op cit* pp 12–14.
24. Sengupta *op cit* pp 155-156; for details of the draft, see The Constitution of the Hindusthan Free State Act, 1944 Archives - Constitution of India.
25. Sengupta *ibid*, pp 165–166.
26. Sengupta *ibid*, p 167.
27. For details, see Constitution of Free India : A Draft (M.N. Roy, 1944) Archives - Constitution of India.
28. For details, see Aundh State Constitution Act 1939 Archives - Constitution of India.
29. For details, see Gandhian Constitution for Free India (Shriman Narayan Agarwal, 1946) Archives - Constitution of India.
30. Granville Austin has discussed in detail why the CA did not accept the Gandhian idea of village-led government. See Austin *op cit* Chapter 2.
31. For details, see A Scheme of Political Safeguards for the Protection of the Depressed Classes in the Future Constitution of a Self-Governing India - A Memorandum by Dr. Ambedkar and Rao Bahadur R. Srinivasan (1930) Archives - Constitution of India.
32. For details, see Communal Deadlock and A Way to Solve It (B.R Ambedkar, 1945) Archives - Constitution of India.
33. For details, see States and Minorities (B.R. Ambedkar, 1947) Archives - Constitution of India.
34. Stages of Constitution Making - Constitution of India.
35. Sengupta *op cit* pp 26–28.
36. *CAD 7-48-226 04 Nov 1948 Archives - Constitution of India.*
37. *CAD* 7–48–227 to 7–48–230 *ibid.*
38. Nehru's speech that includes the text of the resolution can be read at 13 Dec 1946 Archives - Constitution of India accessed on.
39. For more details, see D.D. Basu *Introduction to the Constitution of India* (Lexix Nexis Butterworths Wadhwa, 20th Edition Reprint 2012) p 21.
40. Krishnadas Rajagopal, "Supreme Court Upholds 'Secular, Socialist' in the Preamble of the Constitution", The Hindu, 27 November 2024 Supreme Court upholds 'secular, socialist' in Preamble of the Constitution - The Hindu.
41. Ernest Barker Principles of Social and Political Theory (Oxford University Press, 1986), Barker wrote this in his preface to the first edition published in 1951.

42. Rajeev Bhargava, "Introduction: Outline of a Political Theory of the Indian Constitution" in Rajeev Bhargava (ed.) *Politics and Ethics of the Indian Constitution*, (Oxford University Press, 2008), p 37.
43. Granville Austin gives details of how the amending procedure evolved from committee stage to Draft Constitution to the final version. See Austin *op cit* Chapter 11.
44. To read the full speech by Ambedkar, see CAD, Vol , 4 November 1948, 04 Nov 1948 Archives - Constitution of India.
45. *Ibid.*
46. Article 304 of the Draft Constitution Draft Constitution of India 1948 Archives - Constitution of India.
47. The details of the debate on procedure to amend the constitution can be found in CAD 9-143-452 to 9-143-618, 17 Sep 1949 Archives - Constitution of India.
48. Basu *op cit* p 162.

2

Fundamental Rights and Directive Principles

Rights can be defined as claims of individuals which seek to restrict arbitrary power of the state. These claims need to be secured through legal and constitutional mechanism. Some rights are 'negative', in the sense that they prevent the state from doing something. For example, right to property prevents the state from taking away the property of any individual in arbitrary way. On the other hand, there are some 'positive' rights, which require the states to do something. For example, right to fair conditions at work requires the state to make laws for minimum wages, or for fixed hours of work.

Written democratic constitutions include a statement of rights of the people and elaborate procedure to protect such rights. All constitutional drafts prepared by Indians prior to the formation of the Constituent Assembly (mentioned in Chapter 1) contained a statement of rights that included civil, political and also economic rights. The preliminary draft of the constitution prepared by B.N. Rau included rights in two categories, viz. 'justiciable' (that included civil and political rights) and 'non-justiciable' (that included economic rights and a few social rights). The Draft Constitution,1948 (DC-1948) gave separate names to these categories as Fundamental Rights and Directive Principles, respectively.

2.1 FUNDAMENTAL RIGHTS[1]

Fundamental Rights are included in the Part III of the Constitution that includes Articles 12–35. Originally, there were seven fundamental rights in the Constitution. However, after the deletion of right to property in 1978, currently there are six fundamental rights. Among these, some rights 'prevent the State from doing something', so that a certain right is protected. Thus, the Right to Life prevents the State from taking away the life of any citizen; and the Right to Personal Liberty prevents the State from trying a person more than once for the same offence. Some rights, on the other hand, require the State to 'act in order to secure the right' to the people. For example, the Right against Exploitation requires the State to act to prevent trafficking and child labour.

Article 12 deals with the definitions[2] and Article 13 protects the fundamental rights from legislative encroachment. Rest of the Articles confer specific rights.

Box 2.1: Article 12—Definition of 'State'

- Defines what is the 'State' in the context of Chapter III of the Constitution.
- Accordingly, the term 'State', "includes the Government and Parliament of India and the Government and the Legislature of each of the States and all local or other authorities within the territory of India or under the control of the Government of India."
- Mahboob Ali Baig raised objection to the definition during the debate in the CA, saying that the wide definition would mean that even local bodies or "other authorities" could make laws/by-laws or pass orders restricting fundamental rights.
- B.R. Ambedkar justified the wide definition primarily in terms of convenience and brevity.

Box 2.2: Article 13—Protection of Rights from Laws

- 13(1): declares that all laws that existed before the commencement of the Constitution, and are inconsistent with the provisions of Part III, will be void to the extent of inconsistency.
- 13(2): prevents the State from making any law taking away or abridging the rights in Part III; and declares void any law made in contravention with Part III, to the extent of inconsistency.
- 13(3): defines the terms 'law' and 'law in force'.
- 13(4) (inserted by Twenty-fourth Amendment, 1971): nothing in this Article applies to an amendment to the Constitution passed under Article 368.

The specific Fundamental Rights in Chapter III are explained below.

TABLE 2.1 Right to Equality

Article/Right	*Description*	*Amendments*
14: Equality before Law	Ensures Equality before Law and Equal Protection of the Law.	

(Contd.)

Article/Right	*Description*	*Amendments*
15: Prohibition of discrimination on grounds of religion, race, caste, sex, place of birth	Prevents discrimination on grounds of religion, race, caste, sex, place of birth [15(1)] and ensures access to *all* to public places [15(2)]. Enables the State to make special provisions for women and children [15(3)]; for socially and educationally backward classes, for Scheduled Castes and Scheduled Tribes [15(4)]; and special provisions for socially and educationally backward classes, for Scheduled Castes and Scheduled Tribes [15(5)] as well as for economically weaker sections [15(6)], for admissions to educational institutions, public or private.	15(4) inserted by First Amendment, 1951. 15(5) inserted by Ninety-Third Amendment, 2005. 15(6) inserted by One Hundred and Third Amendment, 2019.
16: Equality of opportunity in matters of public employment	Equality of opportunity in public employment [16(1)], irrespective of religion, race, caste, sex, place of birth [16(2)]; Enables Parliament to make 'residence' a condition for employment in a certain state [16(3)]; enables State to reserve seats for backward classes [16(4)]; and for economically weaker sections of citizens [16(6)] in public employment.	16(3) amended by Seventh Amendment, 1956. 16(4A) inserted by Seventy-seventh Amendment, 1995, and amended subsequently by Eighty-fifth Amendment, 2001. 16(4B) inserted by Eighty-first Amendment, 2000. 16(6) inserted by One Hundred and Third Amendment, 2019.
17: Abolition of Untouchability	Abolishes Untouchability and forbids its practice in any form, enforcement of untouchability becomes an offence punishable in accordance to law.	

(Contd.)

Article/Right	*Description*	*Amendments*
18: Abolition of Titles	Abolishes Titles (except the military and academic), prevents citizens from accepting any titles.	

Constituent Assembly Debate

The Draft Constitution of 1948 (DC-1948) had suggested "Protection of Life and Liberty and Equality before Law" as a single right. It was debated as such in the CA. At a later stage, however, the Drafting Committee (DC) decided to split the two rights. Equality before Law was included in Article 14.

Raj Bahadur argued that in addition to the five grounds on which discrimination is sought to be prevented, one more, i.e. 'descent' should be added too.[3] K.T. Shah moved an amendment that sought to enlarge the list of public places where discrimination is prohibited, by adding schools, colleges, places of public entertainment, libraries, parks, gardens, etc.[4] These changes were not accepted.

Alladi Krishnaswami Ayyar proposed an amendment enabling Parliament to make residence in a state a condition for eligibility for certain jobs.[5] This amendment was accepted. The CA also debated whether the term 'backward classes' should be used or more specific terms like scheduled castes be used. The term 'backward classes' was retained.[6]

There was no much debate over abolition of untouchability, reflecting the consensus within the CA over the issue. Regarding abolition of titles, T.T. Krishnamachari, a member of the DC, suggested an amendment, making exception of military and academic titles. This amendment was adopted.[7]

TABLE 2.2 Right to Freedom—Six Freedoms and Restrictions Thereupon

Article	*Freedom of/to*	*Article*	*Restrictions may be imposed*	*Amendments*
19(1)(a)	Speech and expression	19(2)	*In the interest of* sovereignty and integrity of India, *security of the state, friendly relations with foreign countries, public order, morality, contempt of court, defamation, incitement to offence.*	19(2) (entire sub-clause) was substituted by First Amendment, 1951, *with retrospective effect*; underlined words were inserted by Sixteenth Amendment, 1963.

(Contd.)

Article	Freedom of/to	Article	Restrictions may be imposed	Amendments
19(1)(b)	Assemble peaceably and without arms	19(3)	In the interest of sovereignty and integrity of India and public order.	Underlined words were inserted by Sixteenth Amendment, 1963.
19(1)(c)	Form associations or unions or *co-operative societies*	19(4)	In the interest of sovereignty and integrity of India and public order, morality.	Words in *italics* in column 2 inserted by Ninety-seventh Amendment, 2011.
19(1)(d)	Move freely throughout the country	19(5)	In the interests of the general public or for the protection of the interests of any Scheduled Tribe.	
19(1)(e)	Reside in any part of the country	19(5)	In the interests of the general public or for the protection of the interests of any Scheduled Tribe.	
19(1)(g)*	Practise any profession, occupation, trade, business	19(6)	Protecting existing laws in the interest of general public, and *for making necessary professional/ technical qualifications; state-owned corporations can do any trade/ business.*	Words in *italics* were substituted by First Amendment, 1951.

(***Note:** 19(1)(f) was deleted by Forty-fourth Amendment, 1978).

Constituent Assembly Debate

Many members of the CA agreed broadly that rights cannot be absolute and that they are bound to be restricted. However, a significant number of members opposed the restrictions sought to be imposed on the seven freedoms, and did so on varied grounds.

Thus, Hukam Singh observed that whereas in other countries "it is the judiciary which regulates the spheres of these freedoms and the extent of the restrictions to be imposed", in our constitution "it is the legislature that is being empowered with these powers by sub-clauses (2) to (6)".[8] He moved an amendment to delete sub-clauses (2) to (6). Mehboob Ali Beg, while moving his amendment, said "it looks as if the fundamental rights are listed in clause (1) only to be deprived of under clauses (2) to (6)"[9] Damodar Swarup Seth remarked that "under the Draft Constitution we will not have any greater freedom" than under foreign rule; and that "citizens will have no means of getting a sedition law invalidated, however flagrantly such a law may violate their civil rights".[10] He also flagged the danger involved in the President suspending civil liberties under a declaration of emergency. These amendments were not accepted.

Thakur Das Bhargava proposed to introduce the term "reasonable restrictions".[11] K.M. Munshi, a member of the DC, proposed to drop the word "sedition" from the article. These amendments were accepted.[12] T.T. Krishnamachari, another member of the DC, proposed to include the words "contempt of courts" in clause (2). Despite opposition from some members, the amendment was accepted.[13]

TABLE 2.3 Right to Freedom—Life and Personal Liberty

Article/Right	*Description*	*Amendments*
20: Protection in respect of conviction for offences	Conviction only under and punishment not greater than under, the law in force at the time of the act [20(1)]; Protection against prosecution/ punishment more than once for the same offence [20(2)]; Protection against being witness against oneself [20(3)].	
21: Protection of Life and personal liberty	No person shall be deprived of life and personal liberty, except according to procedure established by law.	
21A: Right to Education	State to provide free and compulsory education to children between 6–14 years by making law.	Inserted by Eighty-sixth Amendment, 2002.

(Contd.)

Article/Right	*Description*	*Amendments*
22: Protection against arrest and detention in certain cases	Right to be informed of the ground of arrest and to consult a lawyer [22(1)]; right to be produced before the magistrate within 24 hours of arrest [22(2)]; 22(1) and 22(2) don't apply to enemy alien [22(3)(a)] and to a person arrested under preventive detention laws [22(3)(b)]; restrictions on detention period of those arrested under preventive detention laws [22(4)]; provision regarding disclosing the ground of arrest to those arrested under preventive detention laws [22(5)]; further provisions regarding preventive detention [22(5), (6)]; Parliament to prescribe the maximum period of detention and procedure to be followed by Advisory Board in inquiry [22(7)(b) & (c)].	22(4) and 22(7) were substantially amended by Forty-fourth Amendment, 1978, and the amendment will come into effect on a date to be notified; which is not yet notified.

Preventive detention means imprisoning a person without trial. While this practice is prevalent in many democracies, only in India does it have constitutional sanction.

Constituent Assembly Debate

In addition to some minor changes that were accepted by the CA, Kazi Syed Karimuddin moved an amendment for adding a sub-clause to the right of Protection in Respect of Conviction for Offences. This sub-clause aimed to provide protection against unreasonable searches and seizures.[14] However, this amendment was rejected.

Regarding the right to life and personal liberty, there was a debate over whether to use the term "due process" of law, or to use "procedure established by law". Kazi Syed Karimuddin argued that the latter term would mean the courts will have the right only to see if "the procedure has been complied with", and not the right to "interfere with any law which might have been capricious, unjust or iniquitous."[15] However, Ambedkar responded by saying that *due process* allowed the unelected judges, who themselves are not immune from prejudice, to undermine the authority of the legislature.[16] The phrase "procedure established by law" prevailed in the constitution.

Ambedkar himself brought in an amendment to the Article on Protection against Arrest and Detention, seeking to replace the article in the DC-1948 by a new article. He argued that the new article "turned statutory safeguards for detainees into constitutional guarantees, thereby protecting personal liberty from arbitrary action."[17] An amendment was moved to the new article which gave the accused the right to be defended by a lawyer of own choice. This amendment was accepted.[18] There was a debate on reducing the period of preventive detention.[19] However, these suggestions were rejected.

TABLE 2.4 Right against Exploitation

Article/Right	*Description*
23: Prohibition of traffic in human beings	Prohibition of traffic in human beings, begar and similar forms of forced labour [23(1)]; enables State to impose compulsory services for public purpose, provided that in doing so the State does not discriminate on grounds of religion, race, caste or class [23(2)].
24: Prohibition of employment of children	Prohibits employment of children below the age 14 in factories, mines or any other hazardous employment.

(**Note:** Articles 23 and 24 have not been amended so far.)

Constituent Assembly Debate

K.T. Shah proposed an amendment to the article on Prohibition of Traffic. He wanted the word "devdasi" to be included along with the word "begar".[20] This amendment was rejected.

Damodar Swarup Seth suggested that in addition to prohibiting child labour, the constitution should also prohibit employment of women "at night, in mines, or in industries detrimental to their health." Shibban Lal Saxena supported this amendment.[21] However, this amendment was rejected.

TABLE 2.5 Right to Freedom of Religion

Article/Right	*Description*
25: Freedom of conscience, and of profession, practice and propagation of religion	Subject to public order, morality and health, all persons have freedom of conscience and to profess, practice and propagate religion [25(1)]; enables State to regulate 'secular' activity related to religious practice [25(2)(a)];

(Contd.)

Article/Right	*Description*
	provide for social welfare and reform, and throwing open Hindu public religious institution to all Hindus [25(2)(b)].
26: Freedom to manage religious affairs	Subject to public order, morality and health, religious denomination or section thereof have the right to maintain institutions for religious and charitable purpose [26(a)]; to manage its own affairs in religious matters [26(b)]; to own and acquire property [26(c)]; and to administer such property in accordance with law [26(d)].
27: Freedom of non-payment of taxes for promotion of any particular religion	No person shall be compelled to pay a tax that is meant for payment for promotion of a particular religion or denomination.
28: Freedom not to attend religious instructions in educational institutions	Prohibition of religious instructions in State-funded educational institutions [28(1)]; not applicable to educational institutions under endowment/trust requiring religious instructions, despite being State-funded [28(2)]; no person attending State-funded educational institution shall be compelled to attend religious instructions or worship conducted in that institution [28(3)].

(**Note:** Articles 25, 26, 27, and 28 have not been amended so far.)

Constituent Assembly Debate

Two amendments were moved to the article regarding the freedom to profess, practise and propagate religion. One was moved by Tajamul Hussain, who proposed to drop the word 'propagate' and add 'practise religion privately'.[22] K.T. Shah moved an elaborate amendment that sought to limit the scope of propagating the religion. He said, "the main article gives the right of freedom of propaganda. … My only condition … is that this freedom should not be abused, as it has been in the past."[23] Both the amendments were rejected.

B.R. Ambedkar moved an amendment to the clause on freedom to manage religious affairs. He suggested that the words "subject to public order, morality and health" be inserted in the beginning of the article. This amendment was accepted without debate.[24]

Prohibition of religious instructions in state-funded educational institutions generated several arguments. Mohammed Ismail Sahib said, "It is not necessary for a secular State to ban religious education in State institutions." He argued that imparting religious instructions in state-funded institutions is not against secularism, but compelling a student to study a religion to which he does not belong is against secular nature of the state.[25] Shibban Lal Saxena contended that it should not be forbidden to provide religious education by the state. While agreeing that "minorities should not be compelled to have religious instructions against their wishes"; he argued that the clause is worded in such a way that if the people of the majority "want that their children should have education in their religion, they will not be able to have it if this article is passed."[26] Ambedkar rejected these amendments by pointing out that public funds cannot be used for one particular religion. He was also apprehensive that teachings of one religion could be against that of another, due to which imparting religious instructions in state institutions could lead to conflict in those institutions.[27]

TABLE 2.6 Cultural and Educational Rights

Article/Right	*Description*	*Amendments*
29: Protection of interests of minorities	Right to conserve the distinct language, script, culture of any section of citizens anywhere in the country [29(1)]; right to admission in any State-funded education institution without discrimination on grounds of religion, race, caste, language [29(2)].	
30: Right of minorities to establish and administer educational institutions	Right of religious and linguistic minorities to establish and administer their educational institutions [30(1)]; not violating rights of minority educational institution while compulsorily acquiring its property[30(1A)]; prevention of discrimination by State in granting aid to minority institutions [30(2)].	Article 30(1A) inserted by Forty-fourth Amendment, 1978.

Constituent Assembly Debate

There was a proposal to expand the right to 'conserve' the culture and to also include the right to 'develop' the culture, moved by K.T. Shah. He said that the culture is not static, but is progressive and developing. Thus, it is "more important than conserving it at some stage to which it has risen, is the need to develop it."[28] This was not accepted. Thakur Das Bhargava proposed to amend the right to admission in state-funded institutions, to include the words 'religion, race, caste, language', thus, expanding the scope of the clause.[29] This amendment was accepted.

Damodar Swarup Seth proposed to limit the right to establish and manage educational institutions only to linguistic minorities. His contention was that a secular state should not recognise religious minorities. "Recognition of minorities based on religion or community is the very negation of secularism."[30] This was negated.

An amendment was moved by Z.A. Lari proposing to add a clause to the right to establish and administer educational institutions. This clause provided for a right of children to have primary education in their language and script.[31] Kazi Syed Karimuddin suggested a qualification to this amendment, proposing that this should be done only in case of substantial number of such students being available.[32] Both these amendments were negated.

TABLE 2.7 Right to Constitutional Remedies

Article/Right	*Description*
32: Remedies for enforcement of rights in Part III	Right to move Supreme Court by appropriate proceeding for enforcement of rights [32(1)]; power of the Supreme Court to issue writs, such as habeas corpus, mandamus, prohibition, quo warranto, certiorari [32(2)]; Parliament can empower any other court to exercise the power under 32(2), [32(3)]; the right guaranteed by this article shall not be suspended except as provided in the constitution [32(4)].

A writ can be understood as a formal order by the court. A writ petition is an application filed before the court requesting the court to issue a specific writ. Each writ mentioned in Article 32(2) has a specific meaning and function.[33]

Box 2.3: The Writs—Meaning

- Habeas Corpus: an order calling upon a detaining authority to produce the detainee before the court; to explain the ground of detention to the court and release the detainee if no legal justification found for arrest.
- Mandamus: command to a person to perform a public legal duty which the person has refused to do; and when there is no other mean to make him perform it.
- Prohibition: an order issued by SC or HC prohibiting a lower court to continue proceedings which fall beyond its legal jurisdiction.
- Certiorari: an order to quash the decision of a lower court which goes beyond its legal jurisdiction.
- Quo Warranto: court inquiry into the legality of a claim to public office asserted by a party.

Constituent Assembly Debate

There was near unanimity among members of the CA regarding the importance of Article 32. Yet, a few amendments were moved. H.V. Kamath moved an amendment to drop the specific mention of the writs from clause (2). His contention was, "it is not wise for us nor desirable to lay down what particular writs the Supreme Court should issue in a particular case."[34] Ambedkar responded by saying that through the English jurisprudence, these writs were found to be fool-proof, and hence the DC thought that these "ought to be mentioned by their name in the Constitution without prejudice to the right of the Supreme Court to do justice".[35] The specific mention of writs was retained.

Right to Property

The Constitution as adopted in 1950 included the Right to Property in Article 31. Article 31(1) said that no person shall be deprived of his property save by authority of law. Article 31(2) provided that no property shall be acquired unless the law made for the same either fixes the amount of compensation or sets principles under which compensation will be paid. This Article was the cause of contention between the property owners and the Government. It proved to be a hurdle to the laws abolishing zamindari, and to nationalisation of property/industry. Successive Governments passed Amendments to the Article, or included new Articles that tended to limit the scope of the Right to Property. Finally, the Morarji Desai Government deleted this Article from the Chapter III, by passing the Forty-Fourth Amendment in 1978. The same Amendment added Chapter 4 titled "Right to Property" to Part XII (Finance, Property, Contracts and Suits). It includes a single Article, 300A, which reads as "No person shall be deprived of his property save by authority of law.".[36]

Successive Amendments, beginning with the First Amendment, included Articles 31A, 31B, 31C, 31D to Chapter IV. The purpose of these Articles is to save laws from judicial review. Thus Article 31A saves laws made to abolish zamindari; Article 31B created the Nineth Schedule and provided for inclusion of laws in the Schedule, the purpose of which is to save these laws from judicial review; Article 31C saved laws giving effects to DPs from judicial review; and 31D saved laws in respect of anti-national activity.[37] Article 31C was invalidated by the Minerva Mills judgement, 1980. Article 31D was omitted by the Forty-Fourth Amendment.

2.2 EMERGENCY PROVISIONS AND FUNDAMENTAL RIGHTS

The Indian Constitution envisages various situations which can be called 'emergency', and when it could become difficult to carry on normal functioning of the political system. The Constitution provides special rules of functioning for these 'emergency' situations. The Emergency Provisions directly affect the Fundamental Rights as well as the Federal structure. In this Chapter, the impact of Emergency Provisions on Fundamental Rights is discussed; while the impact on the Federal structure is discussed in Chapter 3.

Provisions about emergency situations are included in Articles 352 to 360 in Part XVIII of the Constitution.[38] The Constitution provides for three types of emergencies: national emergency; emergency within a state, as a result of the breakdown of constitutional machinery in that state; and financial emergency. Articles 358 and 359 provide for suspension of rights and their enforcement during an emergency.

TABLE 2.8 Emergency Provisions

Article	*Description*
352	Power of the President to declare Emergency in case of a threat to security of India by way of war or external aggression or armed rebellion.
353	During an Emergency, the executive and legislative power of the Union will extend to cover the states.
354	Power of the President to make exceptions to provisions regarding distribution of revenue.
355	Duty of the Union to protect states from external aggression or internal disturbance, and to ensure that state governments function in accordance with the provisions of the Constitution.
356	Power of the President to impose President's Rule in any state, if the President is convinced that the government in that state cannot be carried on in accordance with the provisions of the Constitution.
357	Power of the Parliament to confer legislative power in a state (where a proclamation under Art 356 is issued) to the President, and the power of the President to delegate it to any other authority.
358	Suspension of provisions under Art 19 (Right to Freedom) during the Proclamation of Emergency.
359	Suspension of enforcement of Part III (Fundamental Rights), except Articles 20 and 21, during the Proclamation of Emergency.
360	Declaration of financial emergency, and power of the Union Executive to give directions to state governments regarding appropriate financial measures.

Constituent Assembly Debate

Emergency Provisions is a very unique feature of the Indian Constitution, which not only allows the polity to convert from a federal to a unitary structure (as powers of the states can be overtaken by the Union), but also allows it to slip from a democratic into an authoritarian structure (as fundamental rights and their enforcement is suspended). During the debate on Part XVIII in the CA, H.V. Kamath remarked, "I have ransacked most of the constitutions of democratic countries of the world ... and I find no parallel to this Chapter of emergency provisions in any of the other constitutions of democratic countries in the world. ... The closest approximation, to my mind, is reached in the Weimar Constitution of the Third Reich ... But those emergency provisions pale into insignificance when compared with the emergency provisions in this chapter of our Constitution."[39]

K.T. Shah objected to the words "internal disturbance" in Article 352. The term, he argued, is "not only very difficult to define; but the contrast, whatever may be the implication, seems to me to suggest unjustifiable invasion of democratic freedom. The slightest disturbance, slightest fear of disturbance in the internal management of the State, so to say, or any part of it, may entitle the President to declare a State of Emergency, and issue a proclamation on that account."[40]

Shibban Lal Saxena and Naziruddin Ahmad supported the provisions in Article 352.[41] However, Saxena objected to the provision in Article 358 that allows President to suspend rights under Article 19. He felt that if the rights are to be suspended, the power to do so must be given to the Parliament and not to the President.[42] H.V. Kamath went a step ahead and argued that the Article is redundant and should be deleted.[43] P.S. Deshmukh made a similar argument about Article 358 being redundant.[44]

Speaking on Article 359, H.V. Kamath remarked, "The suspension of fundamental rights is not an ordinary matter. It is a very grave matter. I will go so far as to say that it is even graver than the gravest emergency with which the State may be confronted."[45] He moved amendments that required the Presidential order to specify that the enforcement of which rights will be suspended, and also that such order being approved by Parliament with majority. Shibban Lal Saxena proposed an amendment that during Emergency, suspension of enforcement of rights must be done by the Parliament by passing a law to that effect, and not by Presidential order.[46] In a scathing criticism of the draft Article, Saxena said that even the detenus of the 1942 Quit India Movement were able to file habeas corpus petitions to the High Court, and the Courts did hear those petitions. "But in this free India we are providing for the suspension of this most fundamental article". Saxena continued, "I can understand the provision of safeguards for an emergency, but not the complete suppression of the liberty of the citizen. I do not know of any parallel for this anywhere in the constitutions of the world. I, therefore, suggest strongly that this article should be removed from the Constitution; but if that be not possible, I would suggest that my amendment" be accepted.[47] These amendments were, however, rejected.

A Proclamation of Emergency under Article 352 has been made three times.[48] The first two instances were caused by external aggression. A Proclamation was issued by the President in October 1962 due to Chinese aggression; which was revoked in January 1968. The second one was issued in December 1971, during the war with Pakistan. The President also issued an order under Article 359 suspending enforcement of rights in December 1971. This Proclamation was still in operation, when the third one was issued on 25 June 1975, on grounds of *internal disturbance*.

Emergency 1975–1977

Upon the request of Prime Minister Indira Gandhi, President Fakhruddin Ali Ahmed declared Emergency under Article 352 on the grounds of "*internal disturbance*" on 25 June 1975. It remained in effect until 21 March 1977. Simultaneously, Articles 358 and 359 came into effect too, suspending Article 19, as well as the enforcement of all Fundamental Rights under Article 32. This amounted to not only turning a democratic system authoritarian; it also amounted to stripping the citizens of all the Rights.

The suspension of enforcement of rights was challenged in the courts. Many opposition leaders were arrested under the Maintenance of Internal Security Act (MISA). Such leaders approached the HCs filing writ petitions against the arrest. Various HCs, e.g. Delhi, Karnataka, Madhya Pradesh, ordered the release of the applicants. The Indian Government challenged these orders in the SC in what came to be known as the Habeas Corpus Case, 1976.[49] A five-judge bench of SC ruled by a 4:1 majority that during an emergency, firstly, all rights, including the right to life stand suspended under Article 359; and secondly, the right to seek judicial remedy for enforcement of fundamental rights including habeas corpus also stands suspended.[50] This judgement received scathing criticism from all corners.[51]

The Janata Party Government passed the Forty-fourth Amendment in 1976 and amended Article 352. The words 'internal disturbance' as a cause of Emergency were replaced by the words 'armed rebellion". Article 359 was also amended, making Articles 20 and 21 exceptions to provisions of Article 359. It means, the Rights to Life and Personal Liberty will be protected and can be enforced by going to the Supreme Court, even when a proclamation of Emergency is in effect.

Box 2.4: Points to Remember

- In other democracies, Constitutions consider rights as absolute and inalienable, and it is left to the courts to devise restrictions on them. In India, Constitution (and amendments to it) define limitations on rights, and it is left to courts to expand the scope of rights.
- Unlike other democracies, provision for Preventive Detention is a part of the Indian Constitution.
- Protection of Fundamental Rights is also a Fundamental Right. The writs are specifically mentioned in the Constitution.
- India is the only democracy where Constitution includes Emergency provisions. Prior to 1978, all Fundamental Rights including Article 32 could be suspended during an Emergency.

2.3 DIRECTIVE PRINCIPLES OF STATE POLICY

As noted above, the justiciable and non-justiciable rights were separated, first by B.N. Rau and then by the DC-1948. The non-justiciable rights were included in the Constitution in Part IV, as the Directive Principles of State Policy (DPs).[52] It includes twenty articles.[53] The inclusion of DPs in the Constitution was based on two principles, which are embodied in Article 37.[54] Firstly, they were not enforceable in the courts. And secondly, these directives were fundamental to governance.

In the Constituent Assembly, Ambedkar supported the inclusion of DPs because they "were necessary to make India an economic democracy", notes Arghya Sengupta.[55] Granville Austin argues that the DPs "set forth the humanitarian socialist precepts" that were the aim of the "Indian social revolution"; and thus, most members of the CA agreed on their inclusion in the Constitution. He further observes, "almost the only critical voices were those of members who believed that the provisions of the Directives should be justiciable".[56] For example, Rajkumari Amrit Kaur and Hansa Mehta demanded that the Uniform Civil Code is vital to social progress and the Union government must be obligated to enact it within five to ten years.[57]

Part IV combines non-enforceable rights inspired by a variety of political ideologies. Thus, there are rights—indeed majority of them—influenced by Socialist-Marxist ideologies. For example, Article 38, minimisation of income inequalities; Article 39, secure equal pay for equal work; Article 41, Right to Work; Article 45, provide education to all children, etc. Further there are provisions influenced by Gandhian thought; e.g. Article 40, organise and empower Village panchayats as units of self-government; and Article 47, prohibition of consumption of "intoxicating drinks". Besides, there are also some general principles of governance—e.g. Article 49, protection of monuments and places of national interest; and Article 51, secure international peace.

The DPs have not been reduced to mere rhetoric. Over a period, different governments have made laws to give effect to many of the DPs. For example, some state governments passed laws in the 1950's and 1960's introducing institutions of local self-government, giving effect to Article 40. Later, the Indian Parliament passed the Seventy-third and Seventy-fourth Amendments in 1992, making it obligatory to all states to introduce rural and urban local self-governing institutions. Part of Article 41 was given effect by inserting Article 21A in the Part III (see above), thus, making Right to Education a Fundamental Right. Both union and state governments have made laws providing maternity relief to women employees, to give effect to Article 42. State governments have passed minimum wage acts bringing into effect part of Article 43. Some state governments like Uttarakhand and Assam have formulated Uniform Civil Code to give effect to Article 44. Uttarakhand has launched UCC in the State with effect from 27 January 2025. Articles 15(4), 15(5) and 16(4) (see above) have laid the foundation of the policy for reservation of seats for the SCs and STs in government jobs and educational institutions, thus giving effect to Article 46.

Fundamental Duties

There were no Fundamental Duties in the Constitution as enacted in 1950. This part was inserted in the Constitution by the Forty-second Amendment, 1976, passed by the Government of Indira Gandhi during the period of Emergency. Part IV A of the Constitution lists Fundamental Duties of the Citizens. There are eleven duties listed in Article 51A.[58] Fundamental Duties are not enforceable in the courts.

The Janata Party Government led by Morarji Desai dealt with the question of whether the Forty-second Amendment should be repealed entirely, or selectively. The Government consulted several people before drafting the Amendment. One among them was the former Chief Justice of India and Chairman of Law Commission, Justice P.B. Gajendragadkar. According to Granville Austin, Gajendragadkar recommended that the "high-sounding but 'innocuous', Fundamental Duties might be kept."[59] Thus, the Forty-fourth Amendment retained Chapter IV A.

Democratic constitutions do not include duties of the citizens. Instead, they include a statement of rights of the citizens and instruments to limit the powers of the government. None of the various drafts of the constitution prepared by the various Indian parties and leaders (discussed in Chapter 1) included a statement of citizens' duties, the only exception being the Gandhian Constitution.

Today, the Fundamental Duties continue to remain in the Constitution, much less as a Gandhian legacy, and far more as a legacy of the period of Emergency.

2.4 TWO DEBATES: AMENDABILITY AND PRIMACY

In the context of Fundamental Rights, two constitutional debates emerged almost immediately after the Constitution was passed, and even before it was formally adopted. These two debates continued to influence constitutional discourse for nearly three decades. First among these was, given the provisions in Article 13, can Fundamental Rights be amended by the Parliament. The second debate took place around the question of whether the Directive Principles have primacy over Fundamental Rights, or vice versa.

The Question of Amendability of Fundamental Rights

Article 13(2) (See Box 2.2) explicitly protects the Fundamental Rights from legislative encroachment. Despite the explicit provision in Article 13(2), the First Amendment was passed in 1951. The Amendment was challenged in the Supreme Court (SC) in the case known as the Shankari Prasad case. One of the questions raised by the case was whether the Parliament has the power to amend the Fundamental Rights. In its verdict given on 5 October 1951, the SC ruled that the Parliament *has* the power to amend any part of the Constitution under Article 368, *including* the Fundamental Rights.[60] The judgement interpreted that the word 'law' in Article 13 does not include 'amendment'. Thus, by amending the Constitution the Parliament, and by upholding it the SC; established a position that Fundamental Rights are amendable. This position was reiterated by the Sajjan Singh case, 1965; and prevailed until 1967. More amendments were passed to Part III during this period.

However, in 1967, delivering the judgement in the now famous Golaknath case, an eleven-judge bench of the SC overruled this position. It ruled by a 6:5 majority that Fundamental Rights have been given a transcendental position by the Constitution.[61] Hence, Parliament acting under Article 368 does not have the power to amend the Rights. Indeed, it remarked that Article 368 merely lays down the 'procedure' of amendment, and does not confer the 'power' to amend. Further, the judgement interpreted the word 'law' in Article 13 to include an 'amendment' as well. This was a major setback to the government and Parliament. Four years later in 1971, the Parliament passed the Twenty-Fourth Amendment.[62] It added Clause (4) to Article 13, explicitly allowing the Parliament to make an amendment under Article 368 to make changes in the Rights. It also changed the title of Article 368 as "Power of Parliament to Amend the Constitution and Procedure Therefor", thus, nullifying the objection of the Golaknath judgement. Thus, the amendability of Part III was established once again.

The Twenty-Fourth Amendment was challenged in the SC in another landmark case, known as the Kesavananda Bharati case 1973. The SC reversed its position over amendability of Fundamental Rights once again.[63] The case was decided by a thirteen-judge bench which gave its decision by 7:6 majority.[64] The verdict upheld the validity of the Amendment; and restored the pre-Golaknath position, that the Parliament has the power to amend the Constitution including the Fundamental Rights. However, the SC claimed, this power must be exercised within the limitations of the Basic Structure of the Constitution. In the Minerva Mills case, 1980, the SC reiterated, saying, "Since the Constitution had conferred a limited amending power on the Parliament, the Parliament cannot under the exercise of that limited power enlarge that very power into an absolute power. Indeed, a limited amending power is one of the basic features of Indian Constitution and therefore, the limitations on that power cannot be destroyed."[65] This position prevails till date.

Rights and Directives: Debate over Primacy

Beginning with the First Amendment, many amendments were passed in order to give effect to the 'reform' agenda of the Congress Party, which was influenced by the Karachi Resolution, 1931 (discussed in Chapter 1). This included abolition of Zamindari system, as well as promotion of public sector and nationalisation of resources for economic progress.[66] This agenda found support in the DPs, such as, minimising inequality, preventing concentration of wealth, redistribution of the ownership of material resources—mainly, Articles 38 and 39. Thus, the successive Governments not only justified such laws and policies in the name of giving effect to DPs. It was also claimed that the DPs have a priority over the Rights, and that curtailment of a Right cannot be challenged in the court if it is done to implement a DP.

During the 1950's, various State governments introduced laws seeking to abolish Zamindari. Some States nationalised public transport. Later in 1969, the Central Government nationalised private sector Banks; and went on to abolish Privy Purses.[67] These policies obviously resulted in the State overtaking the property of individuals. The affected individuals challenged such laws in the courts. In most cases (if not all), the courts struck down such laws and also emphasised that the aggrieved parties must get adequate compensation for the property seized by the Government. The issue of "fair" compensation for acquired property, however, continued to appear before the courts.[68]

Reaction of Nehru and Indira Gandhi Governments were quite similar to such challenges. Nehru Government added Articles 31A and 31B (by the First Amendment) to protect Zamindari abolition laws from being challenged in the court. Later in December 1954, he introduced a resolution which was passed in the Lok Sabha, declaring "socialistic pattern of society" as the national goal.[69] The Indira Gandhi Government passed the Twenty-Fifth Amendment in 1971.[70] The Amendment added Article 31C, which provided that laws passed to give effect to the DPs cannot be challenged in the court, even on the ground of violation of Fundamental Rights. Later, the Government passed the Forty-Second Amendment, 1976, during the Emergency.[71] This Amendment added Article 31D, which attempted to protect any law giving effect to any DP from being challenged in the court. Thus, the stand-off between the Government and Parliament (claiming superior status to the DPs); and the Judiciary (seeking to establish parity between the Rights and the DPs) went on until late 1970's. Later, the Forty-Fourth Amendment, 1978, deleted Article 31D.

In its decision in the Kesavananda Bharati case, 1973, the SC ruled that the power of the Parliament to amend the Constitution is not unlimited; and the goals of the Welfare State cannot be pursued by affecting freedom and dignity of the individual.[72] The same position was reiterated by the SC in the Minerva Mills case, 1980.[73] The judgement ruled that "the Indian Constitution is founded on the bed-rock of the balance between Parts III and IV. To give absolute primacy to one over the other is to disturb the harmony of the Constitution. This harmony and balance between fundamental rights and directive principles is an essential feature of the basic structure of the Constitution." Thus, the SC has favoured parity of status of the Fundamental Rights and the DPs.

Box 2.5: Points to Remember

- Fundamental Rights are amendable. However, the power to amend of the Parliament is subject to the Doctrine of Basic Structure.
- Despite the obvious difference—i.e., Fundamental Rights are justiciable and Directive Principles are non-justiciable—the judiciary has declared that both are equally important.
- It is the duty of the State to make laws to give effect to Directive Principles. However, such laws cannot be violative of Fundamental Rights, particularly in Articles 14 and 19.

QUESTIONS

Write Short Answers (5 marks each):

1. Explain the limitations on the Right to Equality mentioned in the Constitution.
2. What is Preventive Detention? Mention various laws of preventive detention in India.
3. Briefly explain the importance of the Right Against Exploitation.
4. Describe in brief the protection given to minorities in Cultural and Educational Rights.
5. Bring out the importance of the writs in Article 32.
6. Do you think it is proper to include Fundamental Duties in a democratic constitution? Why?

Answer the Following (15 marks each):

1. Do you think the final form of fundamental rights in the Indian Constitution leans more toward individual liberty or state authority? Write in the context of the Constituent Assembly Debates and support your answer with examples.
2. "Article 19(1) gives freedoms. But Clauses (2) to (6) of Article 19 take away those freedoms." Do you agree? Write your answer with reasons.
3. Examine how the Directive Principles have been implemented through laws, by giving a few examples.
4. Discuss the amendability of Fundamental Rights in the context of the Doctrine of Basic Structure.
5. How did a proclamation of Emergency affect the Fundamental Rights before 1978? Do you think the Rights are more secure even in Emergency after the passing of the Forty-Fourth Amendment, 1978?

PROJECT SUGGESTIONS

1. Conduct a debate/discussion in the class on "Should Directive Principles have priority over Fundamental Rights or vice versa?"
2. Conduct a debate/discussion in the class on "Whether the removal of the Right to Property from the Constitution was necessary for social justice, or it has resulted in weakening individual freedom?"
3. Conduct a debate/discussion in the class on "Censorship".
4. Make a PPT presentation of the Laws that have implemented the Directive Principles of State Policy.

ENDNOTES

1. For the text of the Articles, this section refers to Part III Archives - Constitution of India, and for Amendments, it refers to 2024071689031207 8.pdf (s3waas.gov.in).
2. For the debate over the Article in CA mentioned in Box 2.1, see 25 Nov 1948 Archives - Constitution of India.
3. *CAD* 7-62-95 29 Nov 1948 Archives - Constitution of India.
4. *CAD* 7-62-56 29 Nov 1948 Archives - Constitution of India.
5. *CAD* 7-63-64 30 Nov 1948 Archives - Constitution of India.
6. *CAD* 7-63-152 30 Nov 1948 Archives - Constitution of India.
7. *CAD* 7-63-235 *ibid.*
8. *CAD* 7-64-176 01 Dec 1948 Archives - Constitution of India.
9. *CAD* 7-64-137 *ibid.*
10. *CAD* 7-64-13 *ibid.*
11. *CAD* 7-64-195 *ibid.*
12. *CAD* 7-64-154 *ibid.*
13. *CAD* 10-154-91 17 Oct 1949 Archives - Constitution of India.
14. *CAD* 7-66-11 03 Dec 1948 Archives - Constitution of India.
15. *CAD* 7-67-172 06 Dec 1948 Archives - Constitution of India.
16. To read his complete argument on this point, see *CAD* 7-72-57, 7-72-58 13 Dec 1948 Archives - Constitution of India.
17. See *Summary* Article 22: Protection against arrest and detention in certain cases - Constitution of India.
18. *ibid.*
19. For example, see *CAD* 9-141-92 15 Sep 1949 Archives - Constitution of India.
20. *CAD* 7-66-115 03 Dec 1948 Archives - Constitution of India.
21. *CAD* 7-66-214, 7-66-219 *ibid.*
22. *CAD* 7-66-253 *ibid.*
23. *CAD* 7-66-279 *ibid.*
24. *CAD* 7-68-8 07 Dec 1948 Archives - Constitution of India.
25. *CAD* 7-68-68 *ibid.*
26. *CAD* 7-68-74 *ibid.*
27. *CAD* 7-68-159 to *CAD* 7-68-163 *ibid.*
28. *CAD* 7-69-14 08 Dec 1948 Archives - Constitution of India.
29. *CAD* 7-69-33 *ibid.*
30. *CAD* 7-69-58 *ibid.*
31. *CAD* 7-69-62 *ibid.*

32. *CAD* 7-69-84 *ibid.*
33. For details, see D.D. Basu *Introduction to the Constitution of India,* (LexisNexis Butterworths Wadhwa, 2012), pp 136-140.
34. *CAD* 7-70-56 09 Dec 1948 Archives - Constitution of India.
35. *CAD* 7-70-170 *ibid.*
36. Article 300A: Persons not to be deprived of property save by authority of law - Constitution of India.
37. See the Articles here Part III Archives - Constitution of India.
38. See Part XVIII Part XVIII Archives - Constitution of India.
39. *CAD 9-109-220, 9-109-221* see 02 Aug 1949 Archives - Constitution of India.
40. *CAD 9-109-249* see *ibid.*
41. *CAD* see *9-109-247 to 9-109-253* for Shah and *9-109-258 to 9-109-261* for Ahmad 02 Aug 1949 Archives - Constitution of India.
42. *CAD 9-111-70* see 04 Aug 1949 Archives - Constitution of India.
43. *CAD 9-111-73 to 9-111-76* see *ibid.*
44. *CAD 9-111-78 to 9-111-79* see *ibid.*
45. *CAD 9-111-120* see *ibid.*
46. *CAD 9-111-125* see *ibid.*
47. *CAD 9-111-130* see *ibid.*
48. For details, see Basu *op cit* 360-361.
49. ADM Jabalpur vs Shivkant Shukla Additional District Magistrate, ... vs S. S. Shukla, etc., on 28 April, 1976 (indiankanoon.org).
50. Justices A.N. Ray, M.H. Beg, Y.V. Chandrachud and P.N. Bhagwati formed the majority opinion. The lone dissenting judge was Justice H.R. Khanna.
51. For details, see Brij Kishore Sharma, *Introduction to the Constitution of India* (PHI Learning Pvt Ltd, 2022), pp 71–72.
52. Part IV Archives - Constitution of India.
53. Constitution as adopted in 1950 contained sixteen Articles. Articles 39A, 43A and 48A were inserted by the Forty-second Amendment, 1976; Article 43B was inserted by the Ninety-seventh Amendment, 2011.
54. For text of the Article, see Article 37: Application of the principles contained in this Part - Constitution of India.
55. Arghya Sengupta, *The Colonial Constitution,* (Juggernaught, 2023) p 58.
56. Granville Austin, *The Indian Constitution: Cornerstone of a Nation,* (Oxford University Press, 1966), p 75.
57. Quoted by Sengupta *op cit* p 62.
58. See Part IVA Archives - Constitution of India.
59. Austin (1966) *op cit* p 413.

60. Sri Sankari Prasad Singh Deo vs Union of India and State of Bihar and ... on 5 October, 1951 (indiankanoon.org).
61. I. C. Golaknath & Ors vs State of Punjab & Anrs.(With Connected ... on 27 February, 1967 ; CJI K. Subba Rao and Justices J.C. Shah, S.M. Sikri, J.M. Shelat, C.A. Vaidyalingam and M. Hidaytullah formed the majority view; whereas Justices K.N. Wanchoo, Vishistha Bhargava, G.K. Mitter, R.S. Bachawat and V. Ramaswami formed the minority view.
62. The Constitution (Twenty-fourth Amendment) Act, 1971| National Portal of India.
63. Kesavananda Bharati Sripadagalvaru ... vs State of Kerala and on 24 April, 1973 (indiankanoon.org).
64. CJI S.M. Sikri and Justices K.S. Hegde, Mukherjea, J.M. Shelat, A.N. Grover, Jaganmohan Reddy and H.R. Khanna formed the majority opinion; whereas Justices A.N. Ray, D.G. Palekar, K.K. Mathew, M.H. Beg, S.N. Dwivedi and Y.V. Chandrachud formed the minority opinion.
65. See Minerva Mills Ltd. & Ors vs Union of India & Ors on 31 July, 1980.
66. For details, see Granville Austin, *Working a Democratic Constitution: The Indian Experience,* (Oxford University Press, 1999), pp 70–71.
67. For details, see Austin (1999), *op cit,* pp 78–82 and 215–231.
68. For example, the Bela Banerjee case The State of West Bengal vs Mrs. Bela Banerjee and Others on 11 December, 1953 (indiankanoon.org).
69. Austin (1999), *op cit,* p 107.
70. The Constitution (Twenty-fifth Amendment) Act, 1971, National Portal of India.
71. The Constitution (Forty-second Amendment) Act, 1976, National Portal of India.
72. See Kesavananda Bharati v. State of Kerala (1973) : case analysis.
73. See Minerva Mills Ltd. & Ors vs Union of India & Ors on 31 July, 1980.

3 Federal System

Political systems are categorised as Unitary and Federal depending upon, whether there is a single set of government drawing its authority from the constitution (i.e. Unitary); or there is a dual set of governments—one at the centre and other at the level of the units—both drawing their respective authority from the constitution (i.e. Federal). India has opted for a federal system. One essential element of a federal political system is a 'written' constitution that formally divides powers between federal and state governments. Most federations have a 'rigid' constitution, in the sense that any amendment to the constitution must be passed by the federal as well as the state/provincial legislatures. It is common in a federal constitution to reserve subjects of national importance like foreign policy, defence, currency, international trade, etc., with the federal government; and hand over other subjects like law and order, public health, irrigation, education, etc. to the governments of the states/provinces.

3.1 NATURE AND STRUCTURE OF THE FEDERAL SYSTEM

Article 1(1) of the Constitution of India says "India, that is Bharat, shall be a Union of States."[1] B.R. Ambedkar clarified in his speech, the reason for using the word Union (instead of the word 'federation'). He said, the proposed federation of India is "not the result of an agreement by the States to join in a Federation"; and it "is a Union because it is indestructible."[2]. Indeed, the Indian federal system was a result of a centrally controlled colonial state being converted into a federation by the Constitution.

In his speech presenting the Draft Constitution (DC-1948) to the Constituent Assembly (CA), B.R. Ambedkar argued that there are "two weaknesses from which Federation is alleged to suffer. One is rigidity and the other is legalism."[3] Ambedkar continued, the DC-1948 has introduced certain features that are different from other federations, and that help overcome these two weaknesses.

Box 3.1: Features of Indian Federal System (As Explained by B.R. Ambedkar)

- Works as a federation in normal times; but can be converted to work like a unitary state by a Presidential decree in times of emergency.
- More legislative power is given to the Union than the states.
- Power to amend the Constitution is vested with the Union Parliament and ratification by state legislatures to a constitutional amendment is required only in case of a few provisions.
- There is uniformity of civil and criminal laws across the states.
- There is a single integrated judicial system.
- Without depriving the States of their right to form their own Civil Services; the Indian federal system provides also for a common All India Civil Service.

TABLE 3.1 Indian Federation in Comparative Perspective

India	*Similar*	*Different*
Single Constitution	Canada, Germany	USA, Australia
Single Citizenship	Canada, Germany, Australia	USA
Single Election machinery	—	USA, Canada, Germany
Integrated Judiciary	Canada, Germany, Australia	USA

With many features deviating from the other federal systems, some authors have contended that India's political system is not federal, and have used terms like "quasi-federal" or "statutory decentralisation" to describe the nature of Indian political system. However, Granville Austin prefers to describe it as "co-operative federalism"—a system based on interdependence of federal and state governments and partial dependence of the state governments on the payments from the federal government.[4] Austin further points out that during the *Constituent Assembly Debate*, there were arguments over distribution of powers between the union and state governments, over distribution of sources of revenue, etc. However, there was "relative absence of conflict between" those who wanted more powers for the union government and those who wanted more powers given to the state governments.[5] Louise Tillin describes Indian federalism as "a centralised model with a strong degree of interdependence between the central government and the states."[6]

Evolution of the Units of Federation

The Government of India Act, 1935 suggested a federal system for India for the first time. The process of formation of federal system in India is rather unique and has its roots in the colonial history. Since 1857, British India had two types of administrative units – one, the Governor's Provinces, with the Governor/Lieutenant Governor as the chief executive and having a legislature; and two, the Chief Commissioner's Provinces, which were ruled directly by the Governor-General through the Chief Commissioner, and having no legislature. In addition, there were Princely States, which were more or less autonomous in their internal affairs, but dependent on the British Government for foreign policy and defence. The three types of units had different trajectories of evolution of self-rule under the British Government. The DC-1948 named these units as Part 1 States, Part 2 States and Part 3A and Part 3B States, respectively. Andaman and Nicobar Islands were the only unit in Part 4.[7] These were re-organised under Parts A, B, C, and D and included in the First Schedule of the Constitution.

TABLE 3.2 Evolution of Units of the Federation

Status under the British Rule	*Form of Government under the British Rule*	*Status in the Draft Constitution*	*Since 1950*
Governor's Provinces	Existence of a Legislative Council, Dyarchy in Act of 1919, autonomy and elected Government in Act of 1935.	States in Part 1	States of the Union Territories and names might have changed after reorganisation of states.
Chief Commissioner's Provinces	Ruled directly by the Governor-General through the Chief Commissioner.	States in Part 2	Union Territory (except Delhi); merged later with reorganised States.
Princely States	Ruled by respective Rulers with full autonomy over internal affairs, foreign policy and defence controlled by the British Government.	States in Part 3A and 3B	Merged with reorganised States.

Besides these three types of territories under British rule, there were territories under Portuguese and French rule. These became independent much later. The French colony of Pondicherry was integrated with the Indian Union in 1954; and the Portuguese colonies of Goa, Daman and Diu, Dadra and

Nagar Haveli, in 1961. All of these became Union Territories. Goa became a State later in 1987. Further, after anti-royalist riots in the Kingdom of Sikkim in 1973, and a subsequent referendum; Sikkim was integrated as a State in India in 1975.

Article 2 of the Constitution specifies that the States and the Union Territories will be mentioned in the First Schedule. After independence, boundaries of many States and Union Territories have undergone changes. Some Union Territories have been elevated as States. Article 3 of the Constitution vests the power to make all such changes exclusively in the Parliament. Thus, the First Schedule has gone through many iterations since 1950.[8]

Two Tiers of Government

Federal polity is a dual polity, as mentioned above. In India, the federal government is called as the Union Government. (It is also commonly referred to as the Central Government.) There are two types of units of federation mentioned in the First Schedule, the States and the Union Territories. Thus, the Union Government forms the first tier and the States and the Union Territories form the second tier of the dual federal polity.

TABLE 3.3 Two Tiers of Government

Tier	*Nomenclature*	*Executive*	*Legislature*
Union	Union Government also known as Central Government.	President of India, Union Council of Ministers led by the Prime Minister.	Parliament of India having two chambers, Lok Sabha and Rajya Sabha.
Unit	State Government (Currently, there are 28 States).	Governor, State Council of Ministers led by the Chief Minister.	Legislative Assembly (Vidhan Sabha) 6 out of 28 States also have a second chamber known as Legislative Council (Vidhan Parishad).
Unit	Union Territory (Currently, 3 out of the total 9 UTs have an elected legislature and government).	Lieutenant Governor, Council of Ministers of UT led by the Chief Minister.	Legislative Assembly
Unit	Union Territory (6 UTs)	Lieutenant Governor	None

The Third Tier

In most federal systems, there is also a third tier of government at the local level. Entry 5 in List II: State List in the Seventh Schedule entrusted the subject 'formation and powers of the local government' to the State governments.[9] Much later, in 1992, the Parliament passed the 73rd and 74th Amendments to the Constitution. The Statements of Objects and Reasons of these two amendments observed that, both rural and urban local governments have not proved to be "viable responsive people's bodies"; indeed, they have "become weak and ineffective" on account of many reasons. Thus, invoking the provision of Article 40 (Directive Principles, see Chapter 2), the parliament decided to include in the Constitution certain basic principles that would ensure "certainty, continuity and strength" to local government.[10] These Amendments gave constitutional status to the Third Tier of government, i.e. local government.

TABLE 3.4 Third Tier of Government—Local Government

Rural	*Urban*
District Board Tehsil Panchayat Village Panchayat (Nomenclatures differ from state to state)	Municipal Corporation and Municipal Council

Scheduled Areas, Autonomous Districts

Article 244(1) of Part X applies the provision of the Fifth Schedule to the Scheduled Areas and Scheduled Tribes in States, other than Assam, Meghalaya, Tripura and Mizoram. Article 244(2) applies the provisions of the Sixth Schedule to the administration of tribal areas in the States of Assam, Meghalaya, Tripura and Mizoram.[11] The aim of these provisions is to "protect the interests of Scheduled Tribes with regard to land and other social issues".[12] The history of creating such areas goes back to the British rule, when these areas were governed by the Scheduled Districts Act of 1874.[13]

TABLE 3.5 Administration of Scheduled Areas

Schedule	*Applicable to*	*Provides for*
Fifth Schedule	States *other than* Assam, Meghalaya, Tripura, Mizoram.	• Formation of Tribal Advisory Council (in States having Scheduled Areas and *also* in States not having Scheduled Areas but having Scheduled Tribes); having power to advise the Governor on Tribal matters referred to it by the Governor. • Power of the Governor to exclude the Scheduled Areas from application of any law of the Parliament or of that State Legislature.

(Contd.)

Schedule	*Applicable to*	*Provides for*
Sixth Schedule	Assam, Meghalaya, Tripura, Mizoram.	• Formation of *elected* Autonomous District Councils and Autonomous Regional Councils in areas designated in the Schedule. • Power of these Autonomous Councils to make rules governing various aspects of tribal life, with the approval of the Governor.

Special Provisions under Part XXI

Part XXI includes "Temporary, Transitional and Special Provisions Related to Various States".[14] Article 371A(1)(a) and 371G(a) include special provisions make provisions for the Naga and Mizo people, respectively; for the protection of their religious-social practices and customary law; and administration of justice on the basis of customary law. Article 371A(1)(b) and 371H(a) confer special responsibility on the Governor of Nagaland and Arunachal Pradesh, respectively, with respect to the law and order in the State; and the Governor can act in his discretion in this regard.

Further, Part XXI included Article 370, titled "Temporary Provisions with respect to the State of Jammu and Kashmir". It provided for a separate Constituent Assembly for the State. As stated above, while presenting the DC-1948 Ambedkar had emphasised that the Indian Union will have a single constitution. No province or princely state was allowed to make separate constitution for itself. However, Jammu and Kashmir was the exception to the rule. Further, Article 370(1)(b) limited the power of the Parliament to make laws for the State of Jammu and Kashmir. These provisions under Article 370 were essentially "temporary", as the title of the Article indicated. Hence, Clause (3) of Article 370 also provided for repeal of the Article by a Presidential order. This "temporary provision" continued to exist for nearly seven decades.

The President of India issued an order applying all the provisions of the Constitution of India to the state of Jammu and Kashmir on 5 August 2019. Subsequently, both Houses of Parliament passed the Jammu and Kashmir Reorganisation Bill, 2019, splitting the state into two union territories – Jammu and Kashmir (with a Legislative Assembly) and Ladakh (without a Legislative Assembly). The Parliament further recommended to the President to issue an order to repeal Article 370 by exercising the power given to the President in Article 370(3). The President issued such order on 6 August 2019, thus, ending the special status of the erstwhile state of Jammu and Kashmir.[15]

This order of the President was challenged in the Supreme Court (SC) in Dr. Shah Faesal vs Union of India on 19 August 2019. The SC gave its verdict (on this and many other petitions which were clubbed) on 11 December 2023.[16] It declared that the Presidential orders, applying all provisions of the Constitution to Jammu and Kashmir; and repealing Article 370 as valid.

It must be emphasised that the dual polity of a federal system consists primarily of the central and state governments. However, 73rd and 74th Amendments, as well as the provisions of Part X and Part XXI discussed above do impact the federal system and relations between the Union and States in India. Therefore, it is important to mention these in a discussion of federal system.

3.2 DISTRIBUTION OF POWERS

Distribution of Legislative Powers

Part XI of the Constitution deals with Relations between Union and States.[17] Chapter I of this Part makes provisions for Legislative Relations. Article 246 provides for three Lists with subjects on which the union and the state governments can legislate. This pattern is adopted from the Government of India Act of 1935. The three Lists are given in the *Seventh* Schedule of the Constitution.[18] It may be noted that there was no substantive *debate* on any Article in Chapter I, Part XI in the *Constituent Assembly.*[19]

TABLE 3.6 Division of Powers—Three Lists

List	*Who can legislate*	*No. of subjects in 1950*	*No. of subjects in 2024*
Union	Union Government	97	100
State	State Governments	66	66
Concurrent	Union and State Governments	47	51

TABLE 3.7 Legislative Powers—More to the Union

Article in Chapter I, Part XI	*Description*
245(1)	Parliament can make laws for the whole or part of the territory of India, and the Legislature of a state can make laws for the whole or part of the territory of the concerned state.
248(1)	Vests powers not listed in the Concurrent or State Lists—i.e. residuary powers—with the Parliament.
249	Empowers the Parliament to legislate on any matter in the State List in the national interest.
250	Empowers the Parliament to legislate on any matter in the State List during the Proclamation of Emergency.
251, 254	In case of an inconsistency between the laws made by the Parliament and State Legislature/s, the law of the Parliament shall prevail.

One significant provision that impacts the legislative powers of the States is the power of the Governor to give assent to the bills passed by the State legislatures under Article 200.[20] Under the provision, the Governor of a State may reserve a bill for the consideration of the President.

Article 3 confers another significant legislative power upon the Parliament—the power to form a new state, increase or diminish the area of a state, alter the boundaries of a state or alter the name of a state.[21] It provides further that such bill shall be introduced in the Parliament only on the recommendation of the President.

Distribution of Administrative Powers

Chapter II of Part XI of the Constitution makes provisions for Administrative Relations. It is noted that there was no substantive *debate* on any Article in Chapter II, Part XI in the *Constituent Assembly*.[22] Part XIV of the Constitution makes provisions regarding civil services for the Union and the states.[23] Moreover, Part XVI gives the Union government administrative powers over the Scheduled Areas and Scheduled Tribes in the states.[24] It may be noted that there was no substantive *debate* on these Parts in the *Constituent Assembly*.[25]

TABLE 3.8 Administrative Powers—Union's Regulatory Hand

Article	*Description*
256, 257 (Chapter II, Part XI)	Power of the Union to give directions to state governments in various cases.
258 (Chapter II, Part XI)	Provides the Union government with the power to entrust any function of the Union government to any state government.
262 (Chapter II, Part XI)	Gives the Parliament power to make a law regarding any inter-state river dispute.
263 (Chapter II, Part XI)	Confers on the President the power to appoint an inter-state council to inquire and advise over inter-state disputes, to investigate and discuss subjects of common interest, and to make recommendations for better co-ordination of policy.
Article 312 (Chapter I, Part XIV)	Confers upon the Parliament the power to establish any additional All India Services (including All India Judicial Services) and regulate the recruitment, and the conditions of service of persons appointed, to any such service.
Article 315 (Chapter II, Part XIV)	Provides for the establishment of a Public Service Commission for the Union as well as for the states.

(Contd.)

Article	*Description*
Article 339 (Part XVI)	Power of the President to appoint a Commission to report on the administration of the Scheduled Areas and the welfare of the Scheduled Tribes in the States and to give directions to the states in the matter.
Part XVI	Power of the President to notify certain castes/races/ groups as scheduled castes (Art 341)/ scheduled tribes (Art 342)/socially & educationally backward classes (Art 342A) in a certain state.

Distribution of Financial Powers

Constitution has laid down elaborate provisions about the distribution of taxes and non-tax revenue which is based on the Government of India Act, 1935. Chapter I of Part XII makes provisions for levying taxes and distributing the revenue.[26] It may be noted that there was no substantive *debate* on this Part in the *Constituent Assembly*.[27]

TABLE 3.9 Some Important Provisions in Part XII Chapter I

Article	*Description*
265	No tax to be imposed except by "authority of law"—thus, Union and state governments can levy taxes with regard to the subjects in the Union and State Lists, respectively.
266	Explains what forms the Consolidated Fund and Public Account of both, Union and state governments.
267	Explains what is the Contingency Fund of both, Union and state governments.
275	Empowers the Parliament to give grant-in-aid from the Consolidated Fund to such States as Parliament may determine to be in need of assistance.
279A	Inserted by the 101st Amendment in 2016; makes provision for the formation of the Goods and Services Tax Council.
280	Makes provisions regarding the periodical appointment of Finance Commission of India, that determines the distribution of revenues between the Union and state governments.
281	Provides that the President will lay down the recommendations of the Finance Commission and action taken thereon to the Parliament.

Thus, it is accepted in the Constitution that the sources of revenue of the state governments may not be sufficient to meet their needs. It provides for transfer of money from the Union to state governments in two major ways. One is to distribute tax revenue between the Union and states; and secondly, to extend grants-in-aid to state governments. Hence, the provision for the Finance Commission.

Box 3.2: Finance Commission

- An autonomous body created under Article 280.
- Has the power to make recommendations to the President regarding: (a) what proportion of Union revenues to be transferred to the state governments; and (b) which state should get how much of that revenue
- The Finance Commission (Miscellaneous Provisions) Act, 1951 has made provisions regarding qualifications, disqualifications, term of office, salaries of members.
- Each Finance Commission is appointed to make recommendations for a period of five years and under different terms of reference.
- Fifteen Finance Commissions have completed their respective term so far. The Sixteenth Finance Commission has been appointed in December 2023.
- The Finance Commissions have laid down principles for distribution of revenue, and also for extending grants-in-aid to states.

Taxes are the main source of revenue of the government. Both tiers of government (i.e. Union and States) levy taxes. D.D. Basu classifies the types of revenue sources of the Union and states as shown in the Box below.[28]

Box 3.3: Types of Revenue Sources of Union and State Governments

- Taxes belonging to the Union exclusively.
- Taxes belonging to the states exclusively.
- Taxes levied by Union; but collected and appropriated by states.
- Taxes levied and appropriated by Union; but assigned to states within which they are leviable.
- Taxes levied and collected by Union; and distributed between Union and states.
- Non-tax revenue of the Union.
- Non-tax revenue of the states.

The Goods and Services Tax (GST) and Federal System

The idea of a single common tax on goods and services goes back to the 1980's. The Governments of Rajiv Gandhi and Narasimha Rao initiated a discussion on such tax. In 1999, the Vajpayee Government appointed a committee—headed by Asim Dasgupta, the then Finance Minister of West Bengal—to prepare a model GST. In 2005, the Vijay Kelkar Committee appointed by Vajpayee Government recommended the roll out of GST. Subsequently, the Manmohan Singh Government introduced the One Hundred and Fifteenth Amendment in 2011 to facilitate the introduction of GST. The Bill was referred to the Standing Committee of Parliament which submitted its report in 2013. The Bill, however, lapsed after the dissolution of 15th Lok Sabha. Narendra Modi

Government re-introduced the Amendment, which was passed by the Lok Sabha as One Hundred and First Amendment in May 2015. It was passed by Rajya Sabha in August 2016, and was subsequently ratified by the Legislatures of all 31 states. GST was finally introduced on 1 July 2017.

The primary goal of the GST is to simplify the indirect tax system. There existed a multiplicity of indirect taxes—such as excise duty, service tax, central sales tax, etc.—in a complicated tax framework. These taxes were levied at different levels of the supply chain, sometimes leading to 'tax on tax', and ultimately increasing the tax burden on goods and services.[29] The idea of the GST was conceived to do away with these problems.

GST is levied at all stages right from manufacture up to final consumption with credit of taxes paid at previous stages available as setoff.[30] Under the system, only value addition is taxed. The One Hundred and First Amendment added two Articles to the Chapter I, Part XII of the Constitution, 269A and 279A. Article 269A provides that The CGST and IGST is levied and administered by the Union government, while the SGST is levied and administered by the respective state governments.[31] Article 279A provides for the formation of the Goods and Services Tax Council (GST Council). An important function of this body is to make recommendations to the Union and state governments on tax rates.[32]

Box 3.4: Goods and Services Tax

- Destination based tax on consumption of goods and services, in which only value addition is taxed and burden of tax is borne by the final consumer.
- Subsumed 16 (7 central and 9 state) existing taxes.
- Three categories of GST, viz. Central GST (CGST), Integrated GST (IGST) and State GST (SGST).
- CGST and IGST is levied and administered by the Union government, while the SGST is levied and administered by the respective state governments.
- The Goods and Services Tax Council (GST Council) makes recommendations to the Union and state governments on tax rates.

As the GST subsumed some significant revenue earning taxes of the state governments, it was bound to affect them adversely. In addition to loss of revenue, it would also take away a part of autonomy of the states. However, after a long process of negotiations, the Union and the state governments agreed to launch the GST in a way that, on the one hand, compromised the simplicity of tax structure, but on the other hand, protected fair amount of state autonomy. As one researcher pointed out, the Union Government made several concessions to states by—(a) agreeing to a GST design most preferred by the state governments; (b) increasing the states' share in the devolution of Union taxes; (c) agreeing to a generous compensation package; (d) accepting the demand of the states to keep a few revenue-earning products outside the purview of GST, such as petroleum products; and (e) introducing a new institutional mechanism, the GST Council, in the Constitution, through which the Union and the states pool the legislative power to levy the GST.[33]

Planning Commission and NITI Ayog

There is no mention of the Planning Commission (PC) in the Constitution, thus, it is not a constitutional body. It was set up on 15 March 1950, within two months of the adoption of the Constitution and before the First General Election by a Cabinet Resolution. Thus, it was also not a statutory body.[34] As per the cabinet resolution establishing the PC, it was formed to determine the machinery for implementing the Directive Principles (DPs); and, by assessing the national resources, plan for their effective and balanced use.[35] The PC disbursed the 'plan' grants; while the FC disbursed the 'non-plan' or statutory grants. It also approved separate state plans, including plans for state borrowing.[36] PC played a key role in designing and overseeing a vast set of Centrally Sponsored Schemes (CSS) which earmarked certain programs for national development under the form of central and largely conditional, matching grants.

As Swenden and Saxena argue, the PC was "perceived as a de facto arm of the central government, which through grant-making and central and state planning added to the centralization of Indian federalism."[37] The PC had become controversial from the beginning. Granville Austin mentions that Vallabhbhai Patel was against the body.[38] Patel feared that with the formation of the PC, the Cabinet will be relegated to the fringe of national economic policy-making.

Box 3.5: A Critique of the Planning Commission (PC)

- Ignored—skills of State Govts, entrepreneurial spirit of private investors, the immense diversity of the country.
- Problem of co-ordination between PC and Finance Commission (FC)—generated some inefficiencies in the process of grant allocation.
- Plan grants were much greater, thus, PC—a non-statutory, non-constitutional body undermined the autonomy of FC—a constitutional body.
- Centrally Sponsored Schemes (CSS) devised by the PC touched upon areas even in State List, leading to erosion of power of the States.
- Could not adapt, thus, became irrelevant in the period after liberalisation of the economy, i.e. after 1991.

The PC was dissolved on 17 August 2014, by the Narendra Modi Government. A new body was formed by the Government to replace the PC, called the National Institution for Transforming India (NITI Ayog) on 1 January 2015. Shared vision of national development with the active involvement of the states in the spirit of co-operative federalism is at the heart of this new institution.[39] By opening posts to outside experts on contractual hiring, the NITI Ayog is aiming to evolve into a centra think-tank. However, it remains to be "a central political institution subsumed under the authority of the Prime Minister."[40] Structure of NITI potentially favours early inputs from state governments. However, the Prime Minister's Office (PMO) is in firm control of which issues deserve further consideration.

3.3 ISSUES IN FEDERAL RELATIONS

A resentment of various types of centralising forces had begun to emerge in the states in the 1950's and 1060's. However, the resentment grew over a period, following the defeat of Congress party in many state elections and almost simultaneous rise of regional parties. Tensions between the two tiers of government had begun to show since the late 1970's. A series of meetings of non-Congress parties and governments in 1983—in Bangalore, Vijayawada and Srinagar—"initiated a process during which both the conduct of centre-state relations under the Constitution and the distribution of powers in the Constitution" was challenged.[41] After the first meeting in Bangalore, Prime Minister Indira Gandhi announced the formation of a commission to review the centre-state relations in June 1983. The Commission was headed by a retired judge of the SC R.S. Sarkaria, and came to be known as the Sarkaria Commission. It presented its report to the Government of Prime Minister Rajiv Gandhi in 1987. Prime Minister Manmohan Singh appointed in in April 2007, another commission to look into the responsibilities of the Union Government during major communal violence; and also the broader issue of centre-state relations. The Commission was chaired by former Chief Justice of India (CJI) M.M. Punchhi, and it submitted its report to the government in March 2010.

Both Commissions produced voluminous reports running into hundreds of pages.[42] Both of them made various recommendations towards improving the centre-state relations.

TABLE 3.10 Recommendations of the Sarkaria and Punchhi Commissions

Issue	*Recommendation of Sarkaria Commission*	*Recommendation of Punchhi Commission*
Article 356	Documented the misuse for political purpose of the Article—suggested that it should be the 'last resort'—suggested to amend the Article, requiring Parliament's sanction for its use.	Suggested to amend the Article 356, and to bring only troubled area (rather than the entire State) under President's Rule—which should be imposed for maximum three months.

(Contd.)

Issue	*Recommendation of Sarkaria Commission*	*Recommendation of Punchhi Commission*
Article 258	Suggested more delegation of powers of the Union to States (and districts) under Article 258—believed this will promote co-operative federalism.	—
Judiciary	Recommended that HC judges should not be transferred without their will.	—
Concurrent List	Suggested that the Union Government consults the States before legislating on subjects in the List.	Suggested that the Union Government consults the States before legislating on subjects in the List through the Inter-State Council.
Appointment of Governor	Suggested appointment of 'non-political' person as Governor—suggested a fix term for the Governor.	Suggested formation of a committee led by the PM for appointment of the Governor—recommended consulting the CM on the appointment—fixed term of 5 years for Governor, doing away with "during the pleasure of President"—recommended "impeachment" of Governor parallel to that of the President.
Appointment of Chief Minister by Governor	Recommended elaborate 'order of preference' for appointment of CM.	Recommended elaborate 'order of preference' for appointment of CM similar to Sarkaria Commission.
Communal Violence	—	Recommended amendment of the Communal Violence Bill to allow Union Government to deploy central forces without the consent of the State, for a limited period—suggested formation of National Integration Council.

One of the recommendations of the Sarkaria Commission was to create the Inter-State Council under Article 263 of the Constitution. The same was created by the V.P. Singh government—by a Presidential Order issued by President R. Venkataraman—in May 1990.[43]

Box 3.6: Inter-State Council

- Established under Article 263 through Presidential Order 28 May 1990.
- Composition: PM as Chair, all CMs as Members (if State under President Rule, Governor to be on the Council), CMs of UTs with a Legislature and Administrators of UTs without a Legislature, 6 Cabinet Ministers nominated by PM.
- Has a Secretariat headed by a Secretary in GoI.
- Current ISC constituted on 8 November 2024.

Box 3.7: Points to Remember

- Federal structure of India has evolved from British colonial administrative structure.
- Idea of federalism was first introduced by the Government of India Act, 1935. Most features of federal system are adopted from the same Act.
- The federal government is called the Union (or Central) government. There are two types of units of federation, the states and the union territories.
- There are Scheduled Areas and Special Areas, where the Governor has special administrative powers.
- The Union government has more legislative and amendment power, and greater control over the administration and finance; as compared with the state governments.

3.4 EMERGENCY PROVISIONS AND FEDERAL SYSTEM

Provisions about emergency situations are included in Articles 352 to 360 in Part XVIII of the Constitution.[44] Articles 352–354 and 358, 359 are discussed in Chapter 3. Articles 355 and 356 impact on the federal system. These two Articles and also Article 352 (to the extent it affects federal system) will be discussed in this section.

Constituent Assembly Debate

If a Proclamation of Emergency is issued under Article 352, the Union government has power to take over any/all functions of the state governments. Thus, the country would be converted into a unitary system. K.T. Shah called it a tendency that he viewed with "deep misgivings", of "arming the Central Executive Government with excessive authority". He said, the concerned Article incorporates "worse features of centralised authority".[45]

Article 355 makes protecting a state and ensuring that it functions according to the Constitutional provisions, a duty of the Union. Thus, a Proclamation can be issued under Article 356 by the President to discharge the duty given by Article 355.

B.R. Ambedkar justified the inclusion of Article 355 saying that "if the Centre is to interfere in the administration of provincial affairs ... it must be by and under some obligation which the Constitution imposes upon the Centre. The invasion must not be an invasion which is wanton, arbitrary and unauthorised by law."[46] Calling this a "very intriguing provision" and merely a "pious expression on the part of the Union Government"; P.S. Deshmukh argued that such a provision would not be necessary at all, "if we had not provided that the President will have the power even of setting at naught the Constitution by which the existence and the continuance of the unit or the State have been guaranteed."[47]

Article 356 empowers the President to proclaim emergency in a state. This is also commonly known as President's Rule in a state. The Article in DC-1948 said that President shall use such power on receiving a report from the Governor of the concerned state. Ambedkar proposed an amendment giving the power to the President to proclaim Emergency in a state even *without* a report from the Governor.[48] This amendment faced strong objections and criticism from the members of the CA. H.V. Kamath said, the President should be empowered to act only in case the Governor informs him "that an emergency has arisen". He emphasised that allowing the President to act without a report from the concerned Governor will destroy "the scheme of even the limited provincial autonomy which we have provided for in this Constitution"[49] Shibban Lal Saxena also opposed the amendment proposed by Ambedkar, saying, "I feel that by these Articles we are reducing the autonomy of the States to a farce. These Articles will reduce the State Governments to great subservience to the Central Government. They cannot have any independence whatsoever."[50] P.S. Deshmukh called the proposed amendment "a very radical change" which is not "in conformity with federation." He continued, "If you wish to retain the least possible vestige of a Federation, you must not deprive the head of the unit or the state of all authority in such matters ... you are going not only to override the discretion or the power of the Governor who is your own nominee, but you are going to set at naught the Ministers, the Cabinet in the State as well as the State legislatures."[51] Naziruddin Ahmad said, "While the Centre should necessarily have the power to intervene in times of emergency, it should not take the initiative in the matter. The Governor acting in consultation with the Ministers will be in a better position to make the declaration."[52] Alladi Krishnaswami Ayyar, on the other hand, supported the provisions in Article 355 and 356.[53]

Replying to the debate on Article 356, Ambedkar said, "I do not altogether deny that there is a possibility of these articles being abused or employed for political purposes. But that objection applies to every part of the Constitution which gives power to the Centre to override the Provinces." He further said that he expected "that such articles will never be called into operation and that they would remain a dead letter. If at all they are brought into operation, I hope the President, who is endowed with these powers, will take proper precautions before actually suspending the administration of the provinces."[54]

President's Rule under Article 356

Contrary to the expectation of Ambedkar and the likes of him, Article 356 was used very frequently. It was used for the first time even before the first General Election was held. The Interim Government of Prime Minister Nehru imposed President's rule in Punjab on 20 June 1951 and kept the Assembly suspended for nine months.[55] Article 356 was used as many as 132 times until 2020—which is nearly one-and-a-half times the number of years the Constitution is in operation. While many times President's rule is imposed for reasons well within the bounds of the constitutional provisions; there are several instances of Union Government overstepping the boundaries of constitutional power to evoke Article 256.

TABLE 3.11 Use of Art. 356 in the Tenure of Long-Serving Prime Ministers

Name of the Prime Minister and Ruling Party	*Period in Power*	*No. of times used Article 356 during the tenure*
Jawaharlal Nehru (Congress)	1950–1964	06
Indira Gandhi (Congress)	1966–1977 and 1980–1984	51
Manmohan Singh (Congress)	2004–2014	11
Narendra Modi (Bharatiya Janata Party)	2014–till date	09

Two most glaring incidents of misuse of Article 356 occurred in 1977 and 1980 respectively. The Janata Party won the post-Emergency election in March 1977. Within a month, the Morarji Desai Government dismissed Congress Governments in eight states in just two days—29, 30 April 1977. These states were Madhya Pradesh, Rajasthan, Bihar, Haryana, Himachal Pradesh, Odisha, Punjab and Uttar Pradesh. When the Congress Party returned to power in the Centre in 1980, Indira Gandhi did the same thing to nine state governments in February 1980. She dismissed non-Congress Governments in Rajasthan, Bihar, Gujarat, Maharashtra, Odisha, Punjab, Tamil Nadu, Uttar Pradesh and Madhya Pradesh.[56] Importantly, all the seventeen state governments thus dismissed enjoyed majority in the Legislative Assembly at the time of their dismissal.

In addition to these mass dismissals of 1977 and 1980, there are many more examples of use of Article 356 which went beyond the limits of constitutional power. Thus, to give a few examples, the government of Communist Party of India in Kerala was dismissed 31 July 1959 even when it enjoyed majority in the state Legislature. Tamil Nadu faced a controversial dismissal in 1976. At that time, the DMK government led by M. Karunanidhi enjoyed majority, but was dismissed on grounds of corruption—which is not a reason for the use of Article 356. Presidential Proclamations under Article 356 dismissed three state governments in Himachal Pradesh, Madhya Pradesh and Rajasthan, all ruled by the BJP, on 15 December 1992, in the aftermath of the destruction of the disputed structure in Ayodhya.

Supreme Court and Article 356

The mass dismissals in 1977 led to a case in the Supreme Court (SC), known as the State of Rajasthan vs Union of India, 1977. A nine-judge bench gave a verdict that the SC cannot interfere with the exercise of President's authority under Article 356.[57] However, the SC reversed this position in a landmark case known as the S.R. Bommai Case, in 1994. The Forty–Fourth Amendment to the Constitution (1978) and the Sarkaria Commission Report (1988) preceded the dismissal of Bommai Government in Karnataka in 1989—factors that might have made the reversal of SC position possible.

The Janata Dal Government in Karnataka, led by S.R. Bommai, was reduced to minority following defections in the Party. The Chief Minister requested the Governor to call a session of the Legislative Assembly for a floor test of his government. But Governor P. Venkatasubbaiah did not oblige, nor did he explore other alternatives to form a government. Instead, he sent a report to the President informing the loss of majority of the Bommai Government and requesting the imposition of President's Rule. Subsequently, the President issued a Proclamation under Article 356, in April 1989. Bommai challenged this Proclamation in Karnataka High Court. The High Court rejected his petition. Bommai filed an appeal against the High Court decision in the SC.[58]

Before the SC took up the Bommai case for hearing, five other state governments had filed cases challenging dismissal under Article 356 in respective High Courts. The Government in Nagaland was dismissed by Rajiv Gandhi Government by a Proclamation under 356 in August 1988, and an appeal against it was filed in the Gauhati High Court. Similarly, the Meghalaya Government was dismissed in October 1991. As mentioned above, three state governments were dismissed in the aftermath of the destruction of the disputed structure in Ayodhya. The Central Government called upon the Supreme Court to decide the validity of these five other proclamations in the states of Meghalaya, Nagaland, Madhya Pradesh, Himachal Pradesh and Rajasthan; along with the Bommai case.[59] The SC gave its verdict on the case on 11 March 1994.

Box 3.8: Important Points in the Bommai Case Judgement

- The proclamation of President's Rule is subject to judicial review (as provided by 44th Amendment 1978, on grounds of mala fide Intention).
- If proclamation of President's Rule is found unconstitutional and invalid, it will be open to the Court to restore the status quo ante to the issuance of the Proclamation and hence to restore the Legislative Assembly and the Ministry.
- The grounds of serious allegations of corruption against Ministry of State and financial instability are not enough for imposition of President's Rule.

(Contd.)

- Secularism is the basic feature of our Constitution and any measure or action taken by State government for security of this feature can't lead to use of Article 356; the power under Article 356 can't be used to sort intra party problems of ruling party.
- If Ministry of State resigns or dismissed or loses majority then Governor can't advise President to impose President's Rule until enough measures are taken by Governor for formation an alternative Government.
- The power under Article 356 is an exceptional power and to be used only in case of exigencies.

There were more cases against the imposition of President's rule even after the Bommai case. Five important judgements by the SC in different matters challenging the of use of Article 356 are worth a mention.[60]

Box 3.9: Points to Remember

- Governor has more discretionary powers in the Constitution.
- President's Rule can be proclaimed in a state without consulting or having a report from the Governor of the state.
- Contrary to initial expectations, Article 356 has been used many more times. It has also been used for reasons not supported by the Constitution.
- While the judiciary initially ruled that use of Article 356 is not subject to review, it changed its position subsequently. The Bommai Case is the landmark in that direction, where the SC laid down many principles for the use of Article 256.
- Use of Article 356 has been challenged in the SC four times even after the Bommai judgement.

QUESTIONS

Write Short Answers (5 marks each):

1. Differentiate between unitary and federal systems of government by giving suitable examples.
2. What were the different types of administrative units in pre-independence India? What was their respective status under the Constitution?
3. Explain the significance of Articles 2 and 3 in the context of formation of new states and change of state boundaries.
4. Explain the division of legislative powers between the Union and the States.
5. Explain the division of administrative powers between the Union and the States.

6. Elaborate the rationale behind the introduction of the Goods and Services Tax.
7. What are the main points in the S.R. Bommai verdict (1994) of the Supreme Court?

Answer the Following (15 marks each):

1. How does the Indian Constitution attempt to balance central authority with state autonomy? Give examples from the chapter.
2. Compare and contrast the provisions in the Fifth and Sixth Schedules regarding Scheduled Areas. Examine the importance of provisions related to the federal system in Part XXI of the Constitution.
3. Discuss the constitutional and political implications of the abrogation of Article 370 in 2019. Discuss the Supreme Court verdict regarding it.
4. Examine the role and significance of the Finance Commission in the context of distribution of financial powers.
5. Elaborate the role and functions of the GST Council as explained in Article 279A. Critically assess the impact of the GST on the federal structure of India.

PROJECT SUGGESTIONS

1. Conduct a debate/discussion in the class on "The GST Council and co-operative federalism in India".
2. Conduct a debate/discussion in the class on "The Governor is meant to be a bridge between the Centre and the State but often becomes a cause of friction", in the context of Articles 155, 163 and 200.
3. Roleplay or Simulation:
   - Students roleplay as CMs, PM, Finance Minister, etc.
   - Debate on a federal issue like revenue sharing, language policy, or development grants.
   - Record or perform it live as a class activity.

ENDNOTES

1. See Article 1: Name and Territory of the Union - Constitution of India.
2. *CAD 7-48-248,* see 04 Nov 1948 Archives - Constitution of India.
3. *CAD 7-48-211 to 7-48-223,* 04 Nov 1948 Archives - Constitution of India.
4. Granville Austin, *The Indian Constitution: Cornerstone of a Nation,* (Clarendon Press, 1966), p 187.
5. Austin, 1966 *ibid,* p 186.
6. Louise Tillin *Indian Federalism,* (Oxford University Press India, 2019), Chapter 1.
7. I: The States - Constitution of India.
8. For the concerned Articles, see Part I Archives - Constitution of India ; see the First Schedule here Read - Constitution of India.
9. List II: State List - Constitution of India.
10. See The Constitution (Seventy-third Amendment) Act, 1992, National Portal of India for the 73rd Amendment and The Constitution (Seventy-fourth Amendment) Act, 1992, National Portal of India for the 74th Amendment.
11. See Article 244 Article 244: Administration of Scheduled Areas and Tribal Areas - Constitution of India.
12. Ministry of Tribal Affairs ScheduledAreas.pdf.
13. See The Scheduled Districts Act, 1874.
14. For all Articles in Part XXI, see Part XXI Archives - Constitution of India.
15. *Hindustan Times,* 11 December 2023 Article 370 verdict: What does Supreme Court judgment mean for Jammu & Kashmir? Latest News India - Hindustan Times.
16. The bench of CJI Chandrachud, Justices S.K. Kaul, Sanjiv Khanna, B.R. Gavai and Surya Kant gave a unanimous verdict. For details, see Judgement-Abrogation-of-Article-370.pdf.
17. See Part XI Part XI Archives - Constitution of India.
18. Check the Seventh Schedule Read - Constitution of India , Summary notes under each List show that there was debate over each of them in the CA, however, it was more technical than substantive.
19. See Part XI *ibid,* see the Summary notes under each List.
20. Article 200: Assent to Bills - Constitution of India.
21. Article 3: Formation of new States and alteration of areas, boundaries or names of existing States - Constitution of India.
22. See Part XI *ibid,* see the Summary notes under each Article.
23. See Part XIV Part XIV Archives - Constitution of India.
24. See Part XVI Part XVI Archives - Constitution of India.
25. See the Summary notes under each Article.

26. See Part XII Part XII Archives - Constitution of India.
27. See the Summary notes under each Article.
28. D.D. Basu, *Introduction to the Constitution of India*, (Lexis Nexis Butterworths Wadhwa, 2011, 20th edition) pp 336–337.
29. Singh Rahul Sunilkumar, "6 Years of GST", *Hindustan Times,* 1 July 2023, 6 years of GST: Tracing role of Atal Bihari Vajpayee, Vijay Kelkar, P Chidambaram, Arun Jaitley, and others - Hindustan Times.
30. Central Board of Indirect Taxes and Customs (CBIC) Goods & Service Tax, CBIC, Government of India :: Know About GST.
31. *Ibid*; also see Article 269A (Chapter I, Part XII) added by the One Hundred and First Amendment Article 269A: Levy and collection of goods and services tax in course of inter-State trade or commerce - Constitution of India.
32. Article 279A (Chapter I, Part XII) Article 279A: Goods and Services Tax Council - Constitution of India.
33. Chanchal Kumar Sharma, "GST Reforms and Federalism in India", *Indian Federalism Perspectives IFP-10* (Centre for Multilevel Federalism, 2022) IFP10_CKSharma1.pdf.
34. Basu, *ibid,* p 347.
35. Granville Austin, *Working a Democratic Constitution,* (OUP, 1999) p 71.
36. Wilfried Swenden and Rekha Saxena, "Rethinking Central Planning: A Federal Critique of the Planning Commission", *India Review,* Vol. 16, No. 1, 2017, pp 42-65 Swenden_Saxena_IR_2016_RethinkingCentralPlanning.pdf.
37. Swenden and Saxena *ibid.*
38. Austin, 1999 *ibid,* p 618. For the arguments mentioned in Box , see Austin, 1999 *ibid,* pp 618-625; Swenden and Saxena *op cit.*
39. Swenden and Saxena *op cit,* p 15.
40. Swenden and Saxena *ibid,* p 17.
41. Austin, 1999, *op cit,* p 541.
42. For summary of the Sarkaria Commission Report, see Features of Sarkaria Commission Report on union and state relations - iPleaders; and for Punchhi Commission Report, see M.M. Punchhi Commission: report and recommendations - iPleaders.
43. Composition | ISCS.
44. See Part XVIII Part XVIII Archives - Constitution of India.
45. *CAD 9-109-247* see 02 Aug 1949 Archives - Constitution of India.
46. *CAD 9-110-31* see *ibid.*
47. *CAD 9-110-89* see *ibid.*
48. *CAD 9-110-25* see *ibid.*
49. *CAD 9-110-68* see *ibid.*

50. *CAD 9-110-75* see *ibid.*
51. *CAD 9-110-85* see *ibid.*
52. *CAD 9-110-125* see *ibid.*
53. *CAD 9-110-99 to 9-110-105* see *ibid.*
54. *CAD 9-111-49* 04 Aug 1949 Archives - Constitution of India.
55. Austin, 1966 *op cit,* p.
56. A report in *India Today*, updated 17 February 2016, see Use of President's Rule peaked on February 17, 1980: Some facts - India Today.
57. The bench included CJI M.H. Beg, Justices Y.V. Chandrachud, P.N. Bhagawati, P.K. Goswami, A.C. Gupta, S.M. Fazal Ali and N.L. Untwalia. See *Law Insider* State of Rajasthan & Ors V. Union of India (1977) - LAW INSIDER INDIA- INSIGHT OF LAW (SUPREME COURT, HIGH COURT AND JUDICIARY However, The MP High Court had held the proclamation to be invalid and beyond the scope of Article 356. See Shivangi Goel "S.R. Bommai vs Union of India" *Law Times Journal,* 2 October 2019 S.R. Bommai vs. Union of India - *Law Times Journal.*
58. Dharmendra Kumar Singh, "An Analysis of Pre and Post S.R. Bommai Scenario With Reference to President's Rule in States", *International Journal of Humanities and Social Science Inventions*, Vol. 6, issue 6, June 2017, pp 05-14, B0606040514.pdf.
59. Shivangi Goel *op cit.*
60. For details of the background and judgements in each of these cases, see Dharmendra Kumar Singh *op cit.*

4

The Executive and the Legislature

A government has three organs—legislature, which has the power to make laws; the executive with the power to execute the laws and make and execute policies; and the judiciary, having the power to adjudicate laws and deliver justice. A parliamentary system separates the functions of the three organs from each other. But the executive is drawn from the legislature, which means, the members of the Council of Ministers including the Prime Minister are also the members of the legislature. Further, the Council of Ministers represents the majority in the legislature and is responsible to the legislature. In a presidential system, on the other hand, the executive and the legislature are separated from each other. The President and the Minsters are neither the members of the legislature, nor are they responsible to the legislature. In both systems, the judiciary is separated from the other two organs. It is the non-elected organ of government. Separation of powers also ensures that no one organ is subordinate or superior to the other two.

There is another principle that governs the formation of democratic governments, checks and balance. This ensures that no single organ of government transcends the boundaries of its constitutional authority. This is ensured by equipping each organ with some 'check' vis-à-vis the other two organs, so that the 'balance' among the three can be maintained.

Box 4.1: Principle of Checks and Balance

- Legislature vis-à-vis the executive—the power to ask questions, pass the budget.
- Legislature vis-à-vis the judiciary—the power to remove the judges.
- Executive vis-à-vis the legislature—the power to veto laws.
- Executive vis-à-vis the judiciary—the power to make judicial appointments
- Judiciary vis-à-vis the legislature and executive—the power to make a review of laws and executive actions to determine whether they are consistent with the constitution, and declare the same as void if found unconstitutional.

Indian Constitution has provided for the parliamentary form of government, with independent judiciary and checks and balance. This chapter will discuss the Executive and Legislative organs of the Indian Government. The next chapter will discuss judiciary.

4.1 UNION EXECUTIVE

The Executive in India comprises the President, the Vice President and the Council of Ministers (led by the Prime Minister). Provisions regarding the executive are included in the Part V, the Union; Chapter 1, the Executive in the Constitution.[1]

President and Vice President

The Constitution provides for a President (Article 52) and the Vice President (Article 63) of India. It makes detailed provisions for the election, qualifications, removal, etc. of the two.[2]

TABLE 4.1 Election, Term and Qualifications of President and Vice President

	President	*Vice President*
Election	Article 54: By an Electoral College* consisting of 54(a)—elected members of both Houses of Parliament, and 54(b)—elected members of Legislative Assemblies of the States; By a method of proportional representation described in Article 55.	Article 66(1)—By an Electoral College* consisting of elected members of both Houses of Parliament, by a method of proportional representation. Article 64—Vice President to be the *ex officio* Chairperson of Rajya Sabha.

(Contd.)

	President	*Vice President*
Term of Office and vacancy in Office	Article 56(1): term of office 5 years; President eligible for re-election; Vacancy may be created due to— 56(1)(a)—if President resigns, 56(1)(b)—if President is removed from office by impeachment.	Article 67: term of office 5 years; Vacancy may be created due to— 67(a)—if Vice President resigns, 67(b)—if Vice President is removed by a resolution passed by majority in Rajya Sabha and agreed to by Look Sabha.
Qualifications	Article 58(1)(a)—is a citizen of India, Article 58(1)(b)—is 35 years of age, Article 58(1)(c)—is qualified to be elected to Lok Sabha, Article 58(2)—does not hold any office of profit under Government of India.	Article 66(3)(a)—is a citizen of India, Article 66(3)(b)—is 35 years of age, Article 66(3)(c)—is qualified to be elected to Rajya Sabha, Article 66(4)—does not hold any office of profit under Government of India.

**Electoral College means a specifically selected group of voters for a particular election. There are different selected groups of voters to elect the President and the Vice President, as indicated in the Table above.*

Once elected, the President cannot be removed easily from power. The Constitution provides for an elaborate procedure of removing the President, called "Impeachment" of the President.

Box 4.2: Procedure of Impeachment of the President

- Article 61(1)—charge can be framed by either House,
- Article 61(2)(a)—a resolution in either House proposed by at least $\frac{1}{4}$ of the total membership,
- Article 61(2)(b)—and passed by 2/3 majority; after which
- Article 61(3)—the other House to investigate or order investigation of charges,
- Article 61(4)—a resolution that the charges are sustained is passed by the House by 2/3 majority.

Constituent Assembly Debates

B.R. Ambedkar, in his speech introducing the DC-1948 to the CA, clearly explained the nature of the office of the President in India.[3] He said, the place of the President "in the administration is that of a ceremonial device on a seal by which the nation's decisions are made known." Ambedkar added that the "President of the Indian Union will be generally bound by the advice of his

Ministers. He can do nothing contrary to their advice nor can he do anything without their advice."

There was a debate over the method of presidential election. K.T. Shah moved an amendment that suggested direct election of the President.[4] B.R. Ambedkar responded with the argument that the Indian President is only a figurehead, and thus, direct election is not necessary.[5] The amendment was negated. Krishna Chandra Sharma proposed to amend the Article regarding re-election of the same person as President. The Article provided for re-election only once, and Sharma proposed to remove this restriction.[6] This amendment was accepted. K.T. Shah proposed an amendment to the qualifications of the President, saying that if a Minister wishes to contest the Presidential election, he should first resign as Minister.[7] This amendment was not accepted.

Order of Succession to Presidential Office

As per Article 65 of the Constitution, the Vice President takes charge of the office of the President during his absence.[8] In the event of the death, resignation or removal of the President, the Vice President acts as the President until a new President is elected. If the President is unable to discharge duties due to absence or illness, the Vice President discharges the duties of the President until he resumes office. In case both the offices of President and Vice President fall vacant for any reason, the Chief Justice of India acts as the President; and if the Chief Justice of India (CJI) is also not available, the senior most judge of the Supreme Court (SC) takes charge of the President's office.

Council of Ministers

Provisions regarding the Council of Ministers are included in Articles 74 and 75 of the Constitution.[9]

TABLE 4.2 Provisions regarding the Council of Ministers

Article	*Provision*	*Amendment*
74(1)	A Council of Ministers (CoM) to aid and advise the President, *who shall act in accordance with such advice;* <u>President may ask the CoM to reconsider the advice, but advice after reconsideration will be binding.</u>	Words in *italics* inserted by Forty-Second Amendment, 1976; words underlined inserted by Forty-Fourth Amendment, 1978.
74(2)	Whether or what advice was given to President shall not be questioned in any court.	
75(1)	Prime Minister (PM) appointed by President; other ministers appointed by President on the advice of the PM.	

(Contd.)

Article	*Provision*	*Amendment*
75(1A)	Total number of ministers not to exceed 15% of the total membership of Lok Sabha.	Inserted by Ninety-First Amendment, 2003.
75(1B)	A member disqualified under Anti-Defection Law will not be qualified to be a minister.	Inserted by Ninety-First Amendment, 2003.
75(2)	Ministers shall hold office during the pleasure of the President.	
75(3)	CoM to be collectively responsible to the Lok Sabha.	
75(5)	Minister must be a member of one of the two Houses, if not, must be elected within 6 months of appointment as minister.	

Constituent Assembly Debate

Mohammad Tahir moved an amendment to Article 75(1) that would allow the President to use his discretion too.[10] B.R. Ambedkar's response was that the Indian President is a nominal, not the real, head.[11] This amendment was not accepted.

Types of Ministers and Cabinet Committees

There are two types of Ministers in the Council of Ministers in India—the Cabinet Minister and the junior minister, referred to as the Minister of State. A Cabinet Minister is in-charge of one or more Ministries in the Government; while a Minister of State usually assists the Cabinet Minister. The Cabinet is, thus, a sub-set of the bigger Council of Ministers. Sometimes, Ministers of State are given independent charge of a Ministry, but they are not usually a part of the Cabinet.

The Cabinet functions through various Cabinet Committees on which senior Ministers are appointed.[12] The Committees help divide work of the Cabinet. They consider all matters related to their work, make proposals for the consideration of the Cabinet, sometimes even make decisions.

Box 4.3: Cabinet Committees

- There are two types of Committees—Standing Committees (permanent) and Ad Hoc (appointed by the Prime Minister for a specific task).
- Standing Committees consist of Ministers of the concerned Ministries, and also other senior members of the Cabinet.
- Prime Minister is a member of all Committees.
- Important Standing Committees are—Cabinet Committee on Security (CCS), Cabinet Committee on Economic Affairs (CCEA), Cabinet Committee on Political Affairs (CCPA), Cabinet Committee on Parliamentary Affairs, etc.

President, Prime Minister, Council of Ministers

The executive power of the Union is vested in the President by Article 53.[13] However, the President is not the real executive, he is only a nominal executive. As per Article 74(1) (see above), the Council of Ministers, with the Prime Minister as its head, advices the President on discharge of his functions. In the relationship between the President and the PM, the question whether the President has any discretion while doing his functions, has been a matter of debate. During the Emergency, Indira Gandhi Government tried to put to rest this question by a provision in the Forty-Second Amendment, 1976, amending Article 74(1) (see above). The Amendment deprived the President of any discretion by saying that in the exercise of his functions, the President shall act according the advice given to him by the CoM led by the PM. It became mandatory for the President to follow the advice of the CoM. However, the Morarji Desai Government's Forty-Fourth Amendment, 1978, added a proviso to this. Accordingly, the President may require the CoM to reconsider the advice once. However, it is mandatory for the President to follow the advice sent after reconsideration.

Thus, it is clear that even if the executive power is vested in the President, it is exercised in reality by the CoM led by the PM in the name of the President. Thus, the PM and the CoM is the real executive. The position of the President is that of the Head of the State in India's parliamentary system, while the position of the PM is that of the Head of Government. The implication is, powers that are conferred by the Constitution on the President, are discharged by the PM and the CoM in reality, *in the name of* the President.

TABLE 4.3 Powers of the President[14] (exercised in accordance with the advice of the CoM)

Type of Power	*Description*
Appointments	• Ministers in the CoM—Article 75(1) • Judges of the SC—Article 124(2); and HCs—Article 217(1) • Governors of the States—Article 155 • Chief and other Election Commissioners—Article 324(2) • Comptroller & Auditor General of India—Article 148(1); Attorney-General of India—Article 76; etc.
Military	Supreme Command of the Defence Forces of the Union is vested in the President—Article 53(2)
Diplomatic	• Represent the country abroad; • Conduct and execute foreign policy; • Conduct negotiations on behalf of the country; etc.

(Contd.)

Type of Power	Description
Legislative	• Summon and prorogue the Parliament, dissolve the Lok Sabha—Article 85. • Deliver opening address to the Parliament, and address the Parliament otherwise, send messages to Parliament—Article 86. • Nominate members to Rajya Sabha (12)—Article 80(1)(a). • Give prior sanctions to certain bills—Article 117; give assent to bills passed by the Parliament—Article 111; and in certain cases to the bills passed by a State legislature and sent to him by the Governor of that State—Article 201. • Issue ordinances—Article 123.
Other	Grant pardon to criminals convicted for offences—Article 72.

President's Power to Appoint the Prime Minister

Article 75(1) (see above) says that the Prime Minister shall be appointed by the President. In a parliamentary democracy, the leader of the party that has majority in the parliament is usually appointed as the Prime Minister. Thus, the leader of the party that secures majority in the Lok Sabha is appointed as the Prime Minister by the President. This convention does not leave any discretion to the President regarding the appointment of the Prime Minister, so long as there emerges one party/coalition with clear majority in the Lok Sabha. However, the President may have to use his discretion in case when any single party or coalition fails to secure clear majority in the Lok Sabha. The discretion, if any, is limited to appointing the PM in some specific circumstances. It does not exist while appointing other ministers, because in that, the President is bound by the advice of the PM, once the PM is appointed.

In 1989, for the first time since the promulgation of the Constitution, any single party failed to secure majority in the Lok Sabha. The Congress was returned with the largest number of seats, but fell short of majority, and it preferred to sit in the opposition. Hence, President R. Venkataraman invited V.P. Singh, leader of Janata Dal, the second largest party in the House, to form the government. The government was asked to prove its majority in the Lok Sabha subsequently. It did so, with support from outside by the Bharatiya Janata Party (BJP) and the Left Parties. It is because of the election result and the formation of a government by a party not in majority, it is said that the 1989 election marks the beginning of the Coalition Era in Indian Politics.

Similar situation arose again in the elections of 1991, 1996, 1998, 1999, 2004 and 2009. (For data, see Chapter 6) The Presidents followed the convention of inviting the largest party to form the government and prove its majority on the floor of Lok Sabha. Only once did a party fail to prove its majority on the floor—the BJP in 1996. The governments formed in this way in 1991, 1999, 2004 and 2009 also survived the full five-year term.

There is another situation when the President is required to use his discretion—when an existing government falls due to loss of majority. The

President has to find out if there is another party with enough support to form the government. Such a situation arose many times—in 1979, 1990, 1996, 1998. On first three occasions, another party was given a chance to form the government. These governments did not survive full term, leading to early election to Lok Sabha. In 1998, however, the President dissolved the Lok Sabha on the advice of the PM and called for election.

One assumption in appointing the PM is that the person to be appointed is already elected/appointed by the concerned party as its leader in the Parliament. However, on one occasion the President appointed the PM even before he was elected party leader. The President did so by interpreting Article 75(1) quite literally. After the assassination of Indira Gandhi, President Zail Singh appointed Rajiv Gandhi as Prime Minister even before he was formally elected as the leader of the Congress Parliamentary Party.[15]

An important function of the President is to give assent to the bills passed by the Parliament. This also implies the power of the President to refuse assent. This is discussed in detail under the legislative procedure.

Role of the Prime Minister

The PM in a parliamentary system of government is customarily described as "first among equals". He is the leader of the party, the leader of the CoM and also the face of the country in foreign and diplomatic relations.[16]

Box 4.4: Role of the Prime Minister

- Leader of the majority party in the Parliament.
- Select other ministers—allocate and re-allocate portfolios and business in the Council of Ministers (CoM).
- Chairs the CoM—calls its meetings and chairs the same—decides the agenda of CoM meetings.
- Can ask a minister to resign or remove a minister.
- Makes and co-ordinates policy of the government—supervises all Ministries—assisted by the Prime Minister's Office in this function.
- Serves as the link between the CoM/individual minister and the President
- Resignation of the PM results is considered as resignation of the entire government.

It may be observed that while the role and functions of the office remain the same, some PMs have more grip over the government and policy than others. The nature and extent of control of the PM depends on several factors, such as:

- Status of the PM in the party and competition to his position within the party.
- Status of the party in the Parliament in terms of whether it has clear and comfortable majority, whether it is a coalition government, whether the government is supported by some parties from outside, etc.

- Experience of dealing with the bureaucracy, grip over the bureaucracy.
- Personal leadership qualities like ability to take initiative, to lead from front and also to take responsibility for failures.
- The length of time spent in PM's office.

4.2 UNION PARLIAMENT

The Parliament consists of the President and two Houses, namely, the Rajya Sabha (Council of States) and the Lok Sabha (House of the People). Provisions regarding the executive are included in the Part V, the Union; Chapter 2, Parliament, in the Constitution.[17]

TABLE 4.4 Provisions regarding the Parliament

Provision	*Lok Sabha*	*Rajya Sabha*
Composition	Not more than 530 members from States and not more than 20 from Union Territories (UTs)—Art 81(1). Number of members from each State based on population of that State—each State will be divided into territorial constituencies*—Art 81(2).	Not more than 238 members representing States and Union Territories (UTs) + 12 nominated members—Art 80(1). Number of members from each State/UT stipulated in Fourth Schedule—Art 80(2) Members elected by elected members of the Legislative Assembly of the concerned State by proportional representation—Art 8-(4).
Term	Five years, unless dissolved earlier; term can be extended by one year at a time during Emergency—Art 83(2).	House cannot be dissolved—1/3 members retire every two years—Art 83(1).
Qualifications	Citizen of India—Art 84(a); not less than 25 years of age—Art 84(b).	Citizen of India—Art 84(a); not less than 30 years of age—Art 84(b).

**Readjustment of the territorial constituencies, i.e. "delimitation" is discussed in Chapter 6.*

Lok Sabha elections are conducted on the basis of Territorial Representation System, where the country is divided into territorial constituencies and one member is elected from each constituency on the basis of who gets the *maximum* number of votes. Rajya Sabha elections are elected on the basis of Proportional Representation System, where seats won by each party from a certain State are equivalent to the percentage of votes that party has secured.

Each House has its own presiding officers to regulate the business in the House. Besides, there is a provision for separate secretarial staff for each House.[18]

TABLE 4.5 Presiding Officers of the two Houses

Provision	*Lok Sabha*	*Rajya Sabha*
Presiding Officer	The Speaker and the Deputy Speaker—Article 93. Regulate the business of the House.	Vice President of India is the *ex officio* Chairman of the Rajya Sabha—Articles 64 and 89(1); The Deputy Chairman—Article 89(2). Regulate the business of the House.
Election	Both officers to be elected from among its members—Article 93.	Deputy Chairman to be elected from among its members—Article 89(2).
Removal	Speaker and Deputy Speaker may be removed by a resolution—moved with at least 14 days of notice—passed by majority in Lok Sabha—Article 94(c). Cannot preside over the respective House when a resolution for their removal is being discussed in the House.	May be removed by a resolution—moved with at least 14 days of notice—passed by majority in Rajya Sabha—Chairman/Vice President Article 67(b); Deputy Chairman Article 90(c). Cannot preside over the respective House when a resolution for their removal is being discussed in the House.

The Parliament and its members enjoy certain privileges. Constitution ensures freedom of speech for the members of both Houses within the House. Articles 121 and 122 further strengthen the separation of powers.

Box 4.5: Powers, Privileges, etc.

- Article 98—Each House of the Parliament has its own secretarial staff.
- Article 105—No member shall be liable to any proceeding in the court for anything he says in the Parliament.
- Article 118—Each House to make its own rules of procedure.
- Article 121—No House shall discuss the conduct of the judges of the SC and HCs, except during the process of impeachment.
- Article 122—The courts shall not enquire into the proceedings of the Parliament.

Constituent Assembly Debates

Loknath Misra argued in favour of abolition of the Rajya Sabha. He said, "I do not think there is any real need for the second Chamber, nor do I think that it will serve any useful purpose."[19] K.T. Sha moved an amendment to remove the provision for nomination of twelve members on the Rajya Sabha, arguing that the legislative organ should be wholly elected.[20] Laxminarayan

Sahu also argued in favour of doing away with nomination of members on the Rajya Sabha.[21]

Regarding the election to the Lok Sabha, Kazi Syed Karimuddin proposed the system of proportional representation. He thought it would be better in protecting the interests of the minorities.[22] K.T. Shah also supported election by proportional representation saying that it is intended to "as to reflect the various shades of political opinion which after all, should be reflected in your Legislature, if you desire to be really a democratic government."[23] Ananthasayanam Ayyangar, a member of the Drafting Committee (DC) rejected proportional representation as "not practicable".[24] B.R. Ambedkar also opposed proportional representation for Lok Sabha elections. He said, "proportional representation would not permit a stable government to remain in office, because Parliament would be so divided into so many small groups that every time anything happened which displeased certain groups in Parliament, they would, on that occasion, withdraw their support from the Government".[25]

K.T. Shah moved an amendment requiring the duration between two sessions of the Parliament not to exceed three months. He also suggested that the Parliament once summoned and in session, shall continue to remain so during the year.[26] Shah also wanted to introduce a provision whereby the two Houses of Parliament would be empowered to receive petitions or representations from the people.[27] These suggestions were not accepted.

Procedure for Passing the Bills

The Constitution lays down certain rules regarding passing ordinary and money bills in the Parliament.[28] Under Article 118, the Parliament has made (and keeps amending) rules of business in the Houses, which also provide for detailed legislative procedure.[29]

TABLE 4.6 Provisions regarding Ordinary Bills

Article	*Description*
Art 107(1)	Bill can be introduced in any of the two Houses.
Art 107(2)	Bill must be passed by both Houses, either without amendments, or with amendments agreed by both Houses.
Art 107(3)	Bills do not lapse due to prorogation of the Houses.
Art 107(4)	Bill pending in the Rajya Sabha (RS), which is not passed by Lok Sabha (LS), shall not lapse due to the dissolution of LS.
Art 107(5)	Bill pending in LS; or passed in Lok Sabha and pending in RS, shall lapse due to the dissolution of the LS.
Art 111	Bill passed by both Houses will be presented to President for his assent—President may give assent—or President may return the Bill to the Parliament with a message that it may be reconsidered—if the Parliament passes the Bill, with or without amendments, the President shall give his assent.

TABLE 4.7 Provisions regarding Money Bills

Article	*Description*
Art 110(1)	Defines a money bill—in case of doubt on whether a bill is a money bill, the decision of the LS Speaker shall be final.
Art 109(1)	Money Bill must be introduced in Lok Sabha (LS).
Art 109(2)	After being passed by LS, the Money Bill will be sent to Rajya Sabha (RS), which has to respond within 14 days with recommendations, if any.
Art 109(3)	The Bill is deemed to be passed with amendments by both Houses, if LS accepts the recommendations of the RS.
Art 109(4)	Bill is deemed to be passed with amendments by both Houses, even if LS rejects the recommendations of the RS.
Art 109(5)	Bill is deemed to be passed by both Houses, even if the RS fails to return the same within 14 days.
Art 117(1)	Money bills mentioned in Art 110(1) shall be introduced only with recommendation of the President.

Box 4.6: President's Assent to Bills and Veto

- Art 111—A bill passed by both Houses is presented to the President for assent—he may give assent—or may return the bill to Parliament for reconsideration—if returned by the Parliament after reconsideration, with or without amendments, the President has to give assent—this amounts to limited veto over legislation.
- There is no time limit within which the President must give assent/return bill—this also gives a veto to President, known as the "pocket veto", where President neither gives assent nor refuses it.
- President Zail Singh used this veto vis-à-vis the Indian Post Office (Amendment) Bill, 1986—the Bill was later withdrawn by the V.P. Singh Government in 1990.

Committees of the Parliament

The Parliament deals with complex functions involving considerable amount of work, within limited time. "It cannot, therefore, give close consideration to all the legislative and other matters that come up before it. A good deal of its business is, therefore, transacted in Committees of the House, known as Parliamentary Committees."[30] Parliamentary Committees are appointed or elected by the House; or nominated by the Speaker of LS or the Chairman of the RS.

Box 4.7: Parliamentary Committees

- Standing Committees—permanent and regular committees with work of continuous nature—these include:
  - o Financial Committees, e.g. Public Accounts Committee, Estimates Committee.
  - o Department Related Standing Committees—currently there are 24 such committees.
  - o Business Advisory Committee, Committee on Privileges.
- Ad hoc Committees—appointed for a specific purpose—cease to exist when they finish the task assigned to them and submit a report, e.g. Select and Joint Committees on Bills.

Anti-defection Law and its Impact

The Fifty-Second Amendment to the Constitution, popularly also known as the Anti-defection Law, was passed by the Parliament in 1985. The Bill notes in the beginning that the "evil" of political defections is "a matter of national concern" and seeks to eliminate the same.[31] It amended the Articles related to disqualification of members of Parliament (Article 102) and of the State Legislatures (Article 192), and added the Tenth Schedule to the Constitution. The Tenth Schedule provides for disqualification of members of Parliament and State Legislatures on the grounds of defection, and lists persons exempted from such disqualification. It further says that the decision of the Speaker/Chairman of the House in this case shall be final. It also says that "no court shall have any jurisdiction in respect of any matter connected with the disqualification of a member of a House under this Schedule." Subsequently, the Ninety-First Amendment, 2003 amended certain provisions in the Anti-Defection Law.[32] Exemption of disqualification on the ground of 'split' was deleted by this Amendment.

The Law has fallen short of achieving its main objective, i.e. preventing political defections. However, it has impacted the role of the presiding officers of the Houses of Parliament as well as the State Legislatures.[33]

Box 4.8: Impact of the Anti-defection Law

- Adverse impact on the freedom of speech of members of the Houses—adverse impact also on their voting right.
- Controversies over the decisions of the presiding officers in disqualification of members under Tenth Schedule—accused misuse and politicisation of the office.
- In Kihota Hollohon case, 1992, the five-judge SC bench headed by Justice Venkatachallaiah ruled that the decision of the presiding officer regarding disqualification shall be subject to judicial review.
- The five-judge SC bench verdict in D. Rajendra Singh Rana case, 2007 clarified, if presiding officer fails to act on a complaint or accepts claims of splits and mergers without making a finding, the decision will be subject to judicial review.

Decline of Parliament?

The institution of Parliament in India has been subject of criticism for nearly four decades. People have talked about the 'decline' of the Parliament as an institution of democracy. One researcher argues that the Parliament is "failing as a platform for aggregating citizen preferences into public policy'; due to which "institutional 'shortcuts' to achieve policy change without legislation or legislative oversight seem to be increasingly accepted."[34] She thinks that there is a link between India's parliamentary rules and the observed absenteeism, curtailed debate and frequent disruptions in the Houses of Parliament. Devesh Kapur and Pratap Mehta point out some specific problems: (a) delegation of policy-making authority from Parliament (and executive) to non-statutory bodies, necessitated by the requirement of high level of technical expertise; and (b) courts playing unprecedented governing role and holding parliament's acts to greater scrutiny well beyond areas pertaining to the court's core jurisdiction.[35] They, however, agree that parliamentary democracy remains robust in India, despite significant institutional challenges facing the Parliament.

4.3 THE GOVERNOR OF THE STATE

The second tier of government in the federal structure in India is the State Government. Provisions regarding The States are included in Part VI of the Constitution, which includes provisions about the Executive (Chapter 2), the Legislature (Chapter 3) and the High Courts (HCs—Chapter 5). Organisation of the government in the States is almost the replica of the Union Government. Thus, each State has an Executive, comprising the Governor and the Council of Ministers led by the Chief Minister. The legislature of a State includes the Governor and the Legislative Assembly; and the Legislative Council wherever it exists. Due to the similarities between the CoM in the Union and in the States, as well as between the Parliament and the State Legislative Assemblies; the executive and legislative organs in the States are not discussed in this book. As the Judiciary in India is single integrated judiciary, the Supreme Court and High Courts are discussed together in the same chapter, i.e. Chapter 5.

However, there is one difference between the two tiers of governments—the role of the Governor in a State and that of the President in the Union, is parallel but far from being the same. This is the reason why the office of Governor is discussed in this chapter. The unique position of the Governor, explained below, makes him a key link as well as a controversial factor in the Centre-State relations.

TABLE 4.8 Constitutional Provisions regarding the Governor

Provision	*Description*
Appointment—Article 155	Appointed by the President.
Term of office and vacancy—Article 156	Remains in office "during the pleasure of the President"—156(1). May resign—156(2). Subject to clauses (1) & (2), term of office of Governor to be five years—156(3).
Qualifications—Article 157.	Must be a citizen of India. At least 35 years of age.

TABLE 4.9 Powers of the Governor

Type of Power	*Description*
Appointments	Other Ministers in the CoM, on advice of the CM—Article 164(1). District Judges, in consultation with the HC of the State—Article 233(1).
Legislative	Summon and prorogue the House/s, dissolve the Legislative Assembly—Article 174. Deliver opening address to the Legislature, and address the Legislature otherwise, send messages to Legislature—Article 175. Give assent to bills passed by the Legislature, may return the Bill to the Legislature for reconsideration or reserve the Bill for consideration of the President—Article 200. Issue ordinances—Article 213.
Other	Grant pardon to criminals convicted for offences—Article 161.

Constituent Assembly Debate

The original article in the DC regarding the appointment of Governors proposed an elected governor. It suggested two alternatives, one of which direct election the governor; and the other was appointment by President from a panel of names elected by the legislature of the state. Brajeshwar Prasad proposed an amendment suggesting appointment of governor by the President. He argued that, in order to encourage "centripetal tendencies" in the country, the authority of the Government of India must be maintained over the provinces; and that the President should have a choice to appoint anyone, also from outside the state, as governor.[36] HV Kamath pointed out that the method of direct election of governor is incompatible with the parliamentary form of government, hence, he supported the amendment.[37] He also described appointment of governor by

President as the "lesser-most" evil system.[38] Others like Alladi Krishnaswami Ayyar, PS Deshmukh, BG Kher also supported appointed governors. However, Hukum Singh opposed it, saying that the alternative of the legislature suggesting a panel and the President appointing one of them, is "the best between the two extremes of pure election and pure nomination."[39] In the end, the amendment proposed by Brajeshwar Prasad was passed and became Article 156.

H.V. Kamath objected to the discretionary powers of the Governor (Article 163). He moved an amendment proposing to omit the relevant words. Kamath argued, "There is no strong or valid reason for giving the Governor more authority either in his discretion or otherwise vis-a-vis his ministers, than has been given to the President in relation to his ministers."[40] H.N. Kunzru agreed with Kamath on omitting the words regarding Governor's discretion.[41] Shibban Lal Saxena too argued against the mention of discretionary powers. He argued that such powers would be acceptable if the Governor were an elected Governor. But the "nominated Governors who will function during the pleasure of the President" should not be given such powers.[42] T.T. Krishnamachari, Mahavir Tyagi and B.M. Gupta spoke in favour of the provision.[43]

Comparing the Offices of President and Governor

Like the President, the Governor also has the discretion to appoint the Chief Minister in similar conditions—i.e. in case when any single party or coalition fails to secure clear majority in the Legislative Assembly. However, the Constitution gives a few more discretionary powers to a nominated Governor than to the elected (albeit indirectly) President.

Box 4.9: Discretionary Powers of the Governor

- While there is a Council of Ministers headed by Chief Minister to advise the Governor under Article 163, the Article adds, "except where the Governor is required to exercise his functions in his discretion". This is clearly different from Article 74, which mandates the President to act as per the advice of the CoM and the PM.
- Moreover, under the same Article, (163), the decision of the Governor on what is within his discretion is final.
- The Governor has the power to withhold assent to legislation, and send it for the consideration of the President, under Article 200.

The power of the Governor to reserve a bill passed by the Legislative Assembly of the State for the consideration of the President, as well as the power to send a report on the breakdown of constitutional machinery in the State, are two powers that have an impact on Centre-State relations.

Box 4.10: Points to Remember

- The President is the Nominal executive; the Prime Minister and the Council of Ministers is the Real executive.
- The office of the Prime Minister is the most important office in the government.
- The Speaker of Lok Sabha and the Chairman of Rajya Sabha regulate the business of the respective Houses.
- Members of Parliament enjoy certain important privileges, including exemption from court proceedings on what they say in the House.
- Parliament functions through Committees, Standing Committees as well as Ad Hoc Committees.
- Anti-Defection Law has changed the role of the presiding officers of the Houses.
- The office of the Governor of a State, though parallel to that of the President of the Union, has been bestowed with a few more discretionary powers than the President.

QUESTIONS

Write Short Answers (5 marks each):

1. Define the twin principles of "separation of powers" and "checks and balance".
2. Describe the role and functions of the Vice President of India.
3. Explain the process of impeachment of the President.
4. What role do the Cabinet Committees play?
5. Compare and contrast the constitutional powers of the President and the Governor.
6. What is the role of the presiding officers of the Parliament?
7. Explain the key difference between the process of passing the money bill and an ordinary bill.
8. What is Anti-Defection Law?

Answer the Following (15 marks each):

1. What are the powers of the President? Bring out the limitations on these powers in the context of Article 74(1).
2. Discuss the relationship between the Council of Ministers and the Parliament. How does the Parliament ensure the accountability of the Council of Ministers?
3. "The President is the nominal head, while the Prime Minister is the real executive." Discuss in the light of constitutional provisions.

4. Explain the powers of the President and the Governor—(a) to give assent to bills, and (b) to issue ordinance, with reference to the Constitution. What is the controversy over these powers?
5. Bring out the differences in the composition, term and powers of the Lok Sabha and Rajya Sabha.

PROJECT SUGGESTIONS

1. Prepare a PPT presentation on the process of appointment of—(a) the Prime Minister by the President; and (b) the Chief Minister by the Governor. Make a comparison of the powers of the two offices.
2. Prepare podcast with a PPT presentation explaining the Parliamentary Committees, their role and significance.
3. Conduct a debate/discussion in the class on “Anti-Defection Law has failed to achieve its primary objective”.
4. Conduct a debate/discussion in the class on “Has there been a decline of the institution of Parliament in India?”

ENDNOTES

1. Part V Archives - Constitution of India.
2. For provisions related to the President, see Articles 52–62, and Article 72; for Vice President, see Articles 63–71. See *ibid.*
3. *CAD 7-48-199* www.constitutionofindia.net/debates/04-nov-1948/#102890.
4. *CAD* 7-72-5 13 Dec 1948 Archives - Constitution of India.
5. *CAD* 7-72-44 13 Dec 1948 Archives - Constitution of India.
6. *CAD* 7-72-217 13 Dec 1948 Archives - Constitution of India.
7. *CAD* 7-73-37 27 Dec 1948 Archives - Constitution of India.
8. Article 65: The Vice-President to act as President or to discharge his functions during casual vacancies in the office, or during the absence, of President - Constitution of India.
9. Part V Archives - Constitution of India.
10. *CAD* 7-76-105 30 Dec 1948 Archives - Constitution of India.
11. *CAD* 7-73-187 *ibid.*
12. For information on current Cabinet Committees, see Cabinet Committees : Council of Ministers.
13. Article 53: Executive Power of the Union - Constitution of India.
14. For details, see D.D. Basu, *Introduction to the Constitution of India,* (LexixNexix Butterworths Wadhwa, 2012), pp 180–196.
15. For details, see Shubhabrata Bhattacharya, "The President who used pocket veto to stall legislation he didn't agree with", *The Sunday Guardian,* 19 June 2022.
16. See Basu, *op cit*, p 199.
17. Part V Archives - Constitution of India.
18. For Articles mentioned in Table 4.5 and Box 4.4, see *ibid.*
19. *CAD* 7-78-10, 7-78-11, 03 Jan 1949 Archives - Constitution of India.
20. *CAD* 7-78-54, *ibid.*
21. *CAD* 7-78-85, *ibid.*
22. *CAD* 7-79-5, 04 Jan 1949 Archives - Constitution of India.
23. *CAD* 7-79-33, *ibid.*
24. *CAD* 7-79-176, *ibid.*
25. *CAD* 7-79-186, *ibid.*
26. *CAD,* 8-86-151 and 8-86-155, respectively, 18 May 1949 Archives - Constitution of India.
27. *CAD,* 8-88-66 20 May 1949 Archives - Constitution of India.
28. For Articles mentioned in Box 4.5, 4.6 and 4.7, see *ibid.*

29. *Rules of Procedure and Conduct of Business in Lok Sabha,* (Lok Sabha Secretariat, 2019), see Chapter X.
30. Lok Sabha portal Digital Sansad.
31. For details, see The Constitution (Fifty-second Amendment) Act, 1985, National Portal of India.
32. For details, see Bill No.
33. B. Poornima, "Explicating the Contemporary Debates on Anti-Defetion Law in India", *Journal of Polity and Society,* Vol. 11, issues 1 & 2, January-December, 2019, pp 60–74. Legislative-and-Judicial-Treatment-of-the-Principle-of-Non-Refoulement-in-India-A-Critical-Analysis.pdf.
34. Jessica Wallack, "India's Parliament as a Representative Institution", *India Review*, Vol. 7, No. 2, April-June 2008, pp 91–114. Microsoft Word - Parliament_representative.doc.
35. Devesh Kapur and Pratap Bhanu Mehta, "The Indian Parliament as an Institution of Accountability", *Democracy, Governance and Human Right Programme, Paper Number 23,* (UN Research Institute for Social Development, 2006), p 29.
36. *CAD 8-94-176* see 30 May 1949 Archives - Constitution of India.
37. *CAD 8-94-195* see *ibid.*
38. *CAD 8-94-200* see *ibid.*
39. *CAD 8-94-205* see *ibid.*
40. *CAD 8-96-24* see 01 Jun 1949 Archives - Constitution of India.
41. *CAD 8-96-37* see *ibid.*
42. *CAD 8-96-40* see *ibid.*
43. see *ibid.*

5 Judiciary

Judiciary, like legislature and executive, is an organ of government. It comprises a hierarchy of courts from the lowest to the highest court. Judiciary resolves disputes, and administers justice based upon and by interpreting, existing law. In democratic governments having written constitution, the judiciary is entrusted with the function to protect the rights of the citizens, and also to protect the constitution; which it does by interpreting (and reinterpreting) the constitution.

5.1 ORGANISATION OF THE JUDICIARY

In the Indian judicial hierarchy, the Supreme Court (SC) of India is the apex, i.e. the highest court. Below it are the High Courts (HCs) in various states. Together, the SC and HCs are called the 'higher' judiciary. All courts below the HC are known as the 'subordinate' judiciary. There are two types of courts in every district—the District Court, which handles civil matters; and the Sessions Court, which handles criminal matters. Below these are various types of lower courts, at village or municipal level. Chapter VI of Part VI of the Constitution makes provisions regarding the Subordinate Courts. Article 233 provides for appointment of District judges by the Governor of the concerned state, in consultation with the High Court of that state.[1] Article 234 provides for the appointment of other judges in the Subordinate judiciary by the Governor of the concerned state in consultation with the Public Service Commission of that state.[2]

The Supreme Court (SC)

The Constitution includes provisions regarding the Supreme Court of India in Part V, The Union, Chapter IV—Union Judiciary. Article 130 states that the Supreme Court of India "shall sit in Delhi or in such other place or places, as the Chief Justice of India may, with the approval of the President, from time to time, appoint."[3] Art 124 makes provisions for appointment of the judges of the SC, conditions of their service and removal of judges.[4]

TABLE 5.1 Appointment, Qualifications and Removal of Supreme Court Judges

Article	*Description*
124(1)	Supreme Court of India, consisting of the Chief Justice of India (CJI) and other judges, the number of whom is determined by the Parliament by law.
124(2)	President shall appoint judges to the SC after consultation with other judges of SC and HCs, as he may deem necessary; President shall always consult the CJI while appointing other SC judges. All SC judges will retire at the age of 65; or may resign, or may be removed from office as under clause (4).
124(3)	Qualifications of the SC judges: must be a citizen of India; and, (a) a judge of a HC for 5 years, or (b) an advocate of a HC for 10 years, or (c) in the opinion of the President, a distinguished jurist.
124(4)	Judges of SC can be removed by the President only if both Houses of Parliament pass a resolution to that effect by 2/3 majority on grounds of misbehaviour or incapacity.
124(5)	Parliament to make procedure by law for such removal under clause (4).
124(6)	Judges to take oath of office as prescribed in the Third Schedule, administered by the President.
124(7)	Judges of SC not eligible for pleading before any court in the territory of India after retirement.

Chapter IV of Part V also describes the various jurisdictions of the SC.[5]

Box 5.1: Jurisdictions of the Supreme Court

- Original Jurisdiction: such cases go directly to the SC, and no other lower court. These include disputes between (a) Government of India (GoI) and one or more states; (b) GoI, & one or more states on one side and one or more states on the other side; (c) two or more states. (Article 131).

(Contd.)

- Appellate Jurisdiction: over a decision of any High Court (HC), whether in a civil, criminal or other proceeding, if the HC certifies that, (1) the case involves a substantial question of law as to the interpretation of this Constitution (Article 132); (2) that the case involves a substantial question of law of general importance and (3) that the said question needs to be decided by the SC (Article 133); (4) against death penalty given by any HC (Article 134); (5) SC may grant special leave to appeal against any judgement of any court (Article 136).
- Advice to the President: President may seek the advice of the SC on any matter of law or fact, and the SC will give its opinion to the President (Article 143).
- Review of judgements: SC has the power to review the judgements it had given previously, subject to certain rules. (Article 137).

The High Courts (HCs)

Provisions regarding the High Courts are included in Part VI, The States, Chapter V—High Courts in the States. Article 214 says that "There shall be a High Court for each State".[6] Union Territories (UT) do not have a separate HC. Article 230 confers upon the Parliament the power to include (or exclude) a UT in the jurisdiction of the HC of a state.[7] For example, Madras HC also serves as the HC for the UT of Puducherry (in addition to being HC for Tamil Nadu). In some cases, one HC serves as a HC for two or more states. The power to "establish a common High Court for two or more States or for two or more States and a Union territory" is conferred upon the Parliament by Article 231.[8] Thus, Gauhati HC serves Arunachal Pradesh, Mizoram and Nagaland, besides Assam. Some HCs have branches—called 'benches'—in cities other than the main seat of the HC; e.g. Karnataka HC has benches in Dharwad and Kalburgi, in addition to its main seat in Bengaluru. It is also not necessary that the seat of the HC of a state is in the capital city of that state; e.g. the seat of the Uttarakhand HC is not in Dehradun, the capital city, but is in Nainital.

TABLE 5.2 Appointment, Qualifications and Removal of High Court Judges[9]

Article	*Description*
216	High Court to consist of the Chief Justice and other judges, the number of whom is determined by the President.
217	President shall appoint judges to the HCs. All HC judges will retire at the age of 62; or may resign from office. Qualifications of the HC judges: must be a citizen of India; and, has held a judicial office for 10 years, or (b) an advocate of a HC for 10 years

(Contd.)

Article	*Description*
218	The procedure to remove a HC judge from office will be the same as in case of a SC judge, i.e., they can be removed can be removed by the President only if both Houses of Parliament pass a resolution to that effect by 2/3 majority on grounds of misbehaviour or incapacity.
219	HC Judges to take oath of office as prescribed in the Third Schedule, administered by the Governor of the state.
220	A Judge of a HC cannot plead before any court except the SC and other HCs.
221	Salaries and allowances of HC Judges to be determined by the Parliament by law.
222	A Judge in a HC may be transferred by the President to another HC.

Securing Independence of Judiciary

As we have seen in Chapter 4, democratic Governments are organised on the twin principles of 'separation of powers' and 'checks and balance'. Thus, on the one hand, the functions and powers of each organ are carefully separated from each other and on the other, there are checks on the powers of each organ by the other two, thereby maintaining the balance in the government. Written constitutions, therefore, make specific provisions for separating the judiciary from the executive and the legislature, and keeping it independent of executive or legislative control. Indian Constitution is no exception.

There are many provisions in the Constitution that aim to secure the independence of the judiciary. First, Article 145, authorises the SC to make the rules for its own functioning.[10] Clause (5) of this Article requires that the decision of the SC be given by the majority opinion. However, it also empowers the judges in minority to record and deliver their minority judgement. Secondly, the SC (under Article 146) and the HCs (under Article 229) can make appointments of their own officers and servants.[11] And third, Article 227 confers upon the HCs the power of superintendence over all subordinate courts and tribunals throughout the territories within its jurisdiction.[12]

But the most important provision guarding the independence of the judiciary is the procedure for appointment and removal of judges as provided in the Constitution. The Constitution separates the power of appointment of judges and the power of removal of judges. Appointment of all judges are made by the President—judges in the SC under Article 124(2), and judges in the HCs under 217(1). The President is bound to consult the CJI while appointing other judges in the SC; but he is not expected to consult the CJI while appointing judges in the HCs. As seen in Chapter 4, Article 74(1) expects the President to exercise his functions as per the advice given to him by the Council of Ministers. In other words, the President makes appointments of judges on the advice of the Council of Ministers. Article 124 confers the power of removal of judges in the SC upon the Parliament; and Article

218 applies the same provision to the judges of the HCs. No judge can be removed from his office unless such resolution is passed by both Houses of the Parliament by 2/3 majority, and handed in to the President. In other words, the President removes a judge only if so advised by the Parliament by required majority. The power of appointment is vested in the executive, while the power of removal is vested in the Parliament. Thus, B.R Ambedkar said in the Constituent Assembly (CA), these provisions provide a middle course. They do not make the executive "the supreme and the absolute authority in the matter of making appointments". They do not also make the influence of the legislature supreme.[13] Because the executive appoints but cannot remove judges, and the Parliament can remove but cannot appoint judges; neither has complete authority over the judiciary. This secures the independence of judiciary. Whatever authority the executive and the Parliament have vis-à-vis the judiciary, it is an essential part of checks and balance.

Three issues stand out for their significance in the process of evolution of judiciary and judicial practices in India: one, a stand-off over the power of the Judiciary to Judicial Review; two, another stand-off, between the Executive and the Judiciary, particularly with reference to judicial appointments; and three, emergence and proliferation of Public Interest Litigation. Subsequent sections of this Chapter will discuss these issues.

5.2 STAND-OFF OVER JUDICIAL REVIEW

Judicial Review is the power of the judiciary to examine the actions of the legislature, executive and administration, to determine whether those actions are consistent with the constitution, and to declare void any law or a part of it, if found inconsistent with the constitution. In the Indian Constitution, this power of the judiciary is not specifically mentioned. But it is implied; e.g. in Article 13(2), that prevents making of a law to take away or abridge any Fundamental Rights.

It is discussed in Chapter 2 that the SC in the Shankari Prasad judgement (1951) upheld the First Amendment, 1951. This means, the SC upheld Articles 31A and 31B as well as the Ninth Schedule—all three exempting certain acts from judicial review. In a subsequent case, known as the Sajjan Singh case (1965), the SC remarked that the Fundamental Rights were not intended to be beyond the reach of any future amendment.[14] Thus, by and large, it appears that until mid-1960's, the SC had accepted two things—one, the need to implement reforms like Zamindari abolition, therefore, the need to amend the Rights; and two, the Parliament's power to amend the Constitution including the Fundamental Rights. However, the judiciary continued to intervene in cases of property acquisition when compensation was not deemed fair. Thus, it retained its power to review the executive acts of property acquisition. But these interventions were not taken kindly by the Government. The response of the Government and the Parliament to this position of the judiciary is also discussed in Chapter 2.

The SC in the Golaknath case, 1967 ruled that the Parliament has no power to amend the Fundamental Rights.[15] The effect of this ruling was widened scope of judicial review. Two subsequent SC judgements also further widened the power of judicial review, as they struck down the nationalisation of banks (1970) and the abolition of Privy Purses (1971).[16] Indira Gandhi government's response was to pass the Twenty-Fourth and Twenty-Fifth Amendments in 1971.[17] Validity of these amendments was questioned in the landmark Kesavananda Bharati case, 1973.[18]

The Kesavananda Bharati case was decided by a thirteen-judge bench and gave a decision by 7:6 majority.[19] On the one hand, the verdict upheld the validity of the Amendments; and restored the pre Golaknath position, that the Parliament has the power to amend the Constitution including the Fundamental Rights. But on the other hand, and more importantly, the judgement also restored the balance between Parliament's power to amend the Constitution and Judiciary's power to judicial review. It did so through the Doctrine of Basic Structure. It laid down that the Parliament cannot pass an amendment that alters the Basic Structure of the Constitution. CJI Sikri explained five features of the Basic Structure—supremacy of the Constitution, republican democracy, separation of powers, federal structure and secular character of the Constitution. The power of the judiciary was firmly established by the Kesavananda Bharati verdict, as the Doctrine of Basic Structure formed the basis of judicial review.

The SC continued to invoke the Basic Structure in exercise of its power of judicial review in future cases. It was invoked while invalidating Article 329A inserted by the Thirty-Ninth Amendment, 1975 (exempting the Prime Minister and the Speaker of Lok Sabha from election related cases) in the Indira Nehru Gandhi vs Raj Narain case.[20] In the Minerva Mills case 1980, the SC invalidated the section 55 of the Forty-Second Amendment, which exempted all amendments post 1976 from judicial review; and reasserted its power.[21] The SC ruled that even the laws added to the Ninth Schedule were subject to judicial review under the Doctrine of Basic Structure, in the Waman Rao case 1980.[22] Thus, the Doctrine of Basic Structure helped the judiciary reassert its power to judicial review.

5.3 STAND-OFF OVER JUDICIAL APPOINTMENTS

Like most other democratic Constitutions, the Indian Constitution too has conferred the power to appoint judges upon the executive. Over a period, the constitutional provisions have been re-interpreted by, both the executive and the judiciary. While at times the executive was accused of misuse of its power of appointment; the judiciary has evolved a system called appointment by a 'Collegium' which has also proved controversial.

Appointment of Judges—Constituent Assembly Debate

The constitutional provisions of appointing the judges to the SC and HCs, including the CJI and the Chief Justices of HCs, are described above. There was a lengthy debate in the Constituent Assembly before these provisions were adopted. Shibban Lal Saxena proposed an amendment to the provision for appointment of judges by the President; which required 'confirmation' of these appointments by two-thirds majority of the Parliament sitting in a joint session.[23] K.T. Shah moved an amendment adding the Council of States (Rajya Sabha) to the list of persons to be consulted by the President before making appointment of judges.[24] Mahboob Ali Baig suggested that the appointments "be made with the concurrence of Chief Justice of India".[25] Thus he wanted to ensure that the CJI is not only 'consulted', but agrees to the names of the persons to be appointed.

On seeking the concurrence of the Rajya Sabha to judicial appointments, Ambedkar argued that, apart from being cumbersome, "it also involves the possibility of the appointment being influenced by political pressure and political considerations."[26] Regarding the concurrence of the CJI to all appointments, he said, "those who advocate that proposition seem to rely implicitly both on the impartiality of the Chief Justice and the soundness of his judgment." He said, he had no doubt that the CJI will be an eminent person. And yet, he continued, "the Chief Justice is a man with all the failings, all the sentiments and all the prejudices which we as common people have; and I think, to allow the Chief Justice practically a veto upon the appointment of judges is really to transfer the authority to the Chief Justice which we are not prepared to vest in the President or the Government of the day. I therefore, think that is also a dangerous proposition."[27]

Supersession and Transfers

Until 1973, the principle of seniority was followed while appointing the CJI. Transfer of HC judges were made, by and large, with the consent of the concerned judges. This does not mean that there were no controversies or disagreements between the President, the Government and the Judiciary over appointments and transfers.[28] However, constitutional norms were not completely flouted.

The first case of supersession happened in April 1973, when CJI S.M. Sikri retired. President V.V. Giri, acting on the advice of the Government of Prime Minister Indira Gandhi, appointed Justice A.N. Ray, fourth in the order of seniority, as CJI. In the process, the three senior-most judges, Justices J.M. Shelat, K.S. Hegde and A.N. Grover, in that order, were superseded. The three superseded judges resigned immediately. Each of the superseded judges was a part of one or two of the benches, hearing the Privy Purses case, Bank Nationalisation case and Kesavananda Bharati Case. All their decisions in these cases were against the Government's policy. On the other hand, Justice Ray's decisions in Bank Nationalisation case and Kesavananda Bharati case (minority view in both) was in the favour of Government's policy.[29] Later, when Justice Ray retired in January 1977 (during Emergency), once again the President, acting on the advice of the Government, superseded the senior-most Justice H.R. Khanna and appointed Justice M.H. Beg, second in seniority, as the CJI. Notably, Justice Khanna was the lone dissenting voice in the case of Habeas Corpus. He too, resigned after being superseded.[30] A report in the Times of India observes that there have been many cases of supersession for nepotism since 1950. However, "no government after Emergency has flouted the seniority convention".[31]

In addition to supersession, many judges were appointed by the Government during the tenure of CJI Ray. At least a few of these judges were responsible for some controversial developments. One of these judges, Justice V.R. Krishna Iyer gave relief to Prime Minister Indira Gandhi in her appeal against her disqualification by the Allahabad HC. In a case filed by Raj Narain, her opponent during the 1971 general election in the Raebareli constituency, the Allahabad HC had held Mrs. Gandhi guilty of 'corrupt practices' during election, and had struck down her election. Mrs. Gandhi filed an appeal in the SC against this verdict; where Justice Iyer gave a decision that upheld her disqualification as Member of Parliament, but allowed her to continue as the Prime Minister with no right to vote in the Lok Sabha.[32] Later, in the Habeas Corpus case (discussed in Chapter 2), another of these judges, Justice P.N. Bhagawati, went with the majority opinion that held Right to Constitutional Remedies as suspended during the Emergency.[33] Together, Justices Iyer and Bhagawati were also responsible for evolving 'activist' judiciary by establishing the practice of Public Interest Litigation (PIL).

During Emergency, President Ahmed, in consultation with CJI Ray, and on the advice of the Government of Prime Minister Indira Gandhi, ordered transfers of judges and Chief Justices (CJs) of various HCs, many of whom had given decisions against the Government's Emergency policies.[34] They were punished for doing their duty of defending of civil liberties and protecting citizens.

Box 5.2: Controversial Transfers of Judges during Emergency

- Justice Ranganathan and Justice R.N. Aggarwal gave a verdict in the Habeas Corpus Case filed by Bharati Nayar in Delhi HC, maintaining that personal liberty cannot be taken away even under laws of emergency. Justice Ranganathan was transferred to Gauhati HC; and Justice Aggarwal's appointment as additional judge was not extended.
- Justice D.M. Chandrashekhar and Justice Sadananda Swamy were on the Karnataka HC bench that quashed the detention of political leaders opposed to Emergency. Justice Chandrashekhar was transferred to Allahabad HC and Justice Swamy was transferred to Gauhati HC.
- Justice A.P. Sen of the Madhya Pradesh HC gave a decision in the Habeas Corpus Case (ADM Jabalpur Case), ruling that the citizens have the Right to Constitutional Remedies even during Emergency. He was transferred to Rajasthan HC as CJ.

Such politicisation of judicial appointments in the 1970's led to deep apprehension within the judiciary. This apprehension caused the developments which ultimately led to the emergence of Collegium System for appointment of judges.

Collegium System: An Evaluation

As a reaction to supersession, there were demands for changing the procedure of appointment of judges. Jayprakash Narayan wrote to the Prime Minister with an appeal "to appoint an all-party parliamentary committee to make recommendations to Parliament about an appointing mechanism."[35] The Supreme Court Bar Association demanded that a committee of five senior judges of the SC and two members of the Bar be established for appointment of judges, and the recommendations of the committee should be accepted by the government.[36] This suggestion may be regarded as an antecedent to the Collegium System. The actual collegium has evolved through three judgements of the SC in the three so-called 'Judges Cases'.[37]

Box 5.3: Evolution of the Collegium System

- The SC ruling in the First Judges Case (1981), written by Justice PN Bhagwati on the behalf of the Bench, said that "consultation" with the CJI in judicial appointments does not necessarily mean "concurrence". The ruling underscored the importance of the executive involvement in ensuring checks and balances in the appointment process.
- A 9-judge bench of the SC overruled this (1981) judgement by 7:2 majority in 1993, in the Second Judges Case and held that "consultation" did imply "concurrence". It added, "that absolute discretion was not given to anyone, not even to the Chief Justice of India as an individual, much less to the executive". The Court further suggested that the recommendation should be given by a collegium of judges.
- Responding to a Presidential Reference (known as the Third Judges Case), the SC in 1998, further clarified that "the Collegium would comprise the CJI and the four senior-most judges of the Supreme Court."

After 1998, the collegium has been in complete charge of appointing judges; and the authority of the executive to appoint judges has been effectively revoked. However, the shift from "executive appointing judges" to "judges appointing judges" also has its own problems, as is seen from the experience of over twenty-five years of the system.[38] Not only are there serious drawbacks with the functioning of the Collegium System; the fundamental philosophy of the system is not consistent with the conventional understanding of checks and balance.

Box 5.4: Drawbacks of the Collegium System

- Lack of transparency, not only in appointments, but also in transfers. The method of selection, norms of eligibility, etc. are not known in public domain.
- Allegations of favouritism and nepotism are levelled against the Collegium.
- Collegium is contrary to the principle of checks and balance. Denial of a role to executive in judicial appointments amounts to denial of check on and balancing of, the power of judiciary. This is also contrary to the philosophy of the Constitution.
- No other democracy has a system where judges appoint judges.

As explained earlier, out of turn appointments during Emergency were responsible for growing distrust of the executive in the judiciary. In more recent times, the delay in confirming the appointments—for example, that of Saurabh Kirpal as SC judge (Kirpal's name was recommended for the first time in 2017, and three more times since) by the President is shrouded in lack of transparency. While the Government of Prime Minister Modi has cited security concerns raised by the RAW, it is alleged that the appointment is delayed due to the 'different sexual orientation' of Kirpal.[39] On the other hand, as Nahvi and Sharma observe, "the judiciary has strived to increase its power in judicial appointments by reading the Constitution in a way that rewrites it, justifying such transgressions under the garb of interpretation."[40] As the two authors point out, the Indian Constitution had provided for President consulting the CJI in making appointments, where concurrence of the CJI was not a pre-requisite for appointments. This provision was reimagined and almost re-written by the three Judges Cases.

Ninety-ninth Amendment, 2014 and its Invalidation by SC

The Government of Prime Minister Narendra Modi introduced the Ninety-Ninth Amendment Bill in the Parliament seeking to amend the provisions for appointment of SC (Article 124) and HC judges (Article 217), and various related articles. It proposed the formation of a National Judicial Appointments Commission (NJAC) by inserting new Article 124A.[41] The Ninety-ninth Amendment was passed by the Parliament in December 2014.

Box 5.5: National Judicial Appointments Commission (NJAC)

- A six-member Commission to make appointments of WC and HC judges, proposed by the Ninety-ninth Amendment, 2014.
- The six members would be:
  - o CJI as the Chair
  - o two other senior judges of the SC
  - o the Minister of Law and Justice
  - o two eminent persons nominated by a committee consisting of the Prime Minister, the CJI and the Leader of the Opposition in Lok Sabha.
- Amendment struck down by the SC.

The Amendment was challenged in the court by the Supreme Court Advocates-on-Record Association. A five-judge bench of the SC gave its verdict in 2015 by 4:1 majority and struck down the Ninety-ninth Amendment as unconstitutional.[42] The majority judgement held that the NJAC violates the Basic Structure of the Constitution; and held that the need for transparency in judicial appointments must be balanced with the candidates' right to privacy. The verdict reinstated the Collegium System of appointment of judges. However, in his dissenting judgement, Justice Chelameswar pointed various flaws of the Collegium, highlighted the need for transparency in judicial appointments and defended the NJAC as a mechanism that could address the flaws in the Collegium.[43] The Collegium System is back as a result of the judgement in this case, known also as the Fourth Judges Case. However, the stand-off is far from over, as the Government has devised a strategy of delaying appointments of unacceptable names on the list from the Collegium.

5.4 PUBLIC INTEREST LITIGATION (PIL)

Public Interest Litigation (PIL) is a uniquely Indian judicial development. It emerged in the period after Emergency. In simple terms, a PIL can be defined as litigation to protect the interest of the public at large. Normally, a case can be filed in the court *only* by such person/s whose interest is affected—those having *'locus standi'* or 'standing' in the court. PIL, however, can be filed by *any* person, even with no standing in the case, provided such case is filed with the intention to protect or benefit larger interest of the public. The judgement in the First Judges Case (1981) reinterpreted 'standing' and redefined the role of courts.[44] Thus, the Courts assumed a role as a mechanism by which individuals could challenge the failures of government in terms of statutory non-enforcement, violations of the Constitution, or breach of public duty. Petitions filed to that end by *anyone* (i.e., not necessarily having a 'standing' in the case), came to be known as PIL. In a PIL, the courts can issue relief in the form of orders and directives in order to monitor the progress of the case.

A well-known legal expert noted three important factors that contributed to the emergence of PIL.[45] These, he calls, judicial populism, Emergency populism and nexus with the Press. Another expert traces the origins of PIL to the two reports on the functioning of the judiciary, submitted by the two commissions appointed by the Indira Gandhi government.[46] The first of these was the report of the Experts Committee on Legal Aid, Chaired by Justice Krishna Iyer and submitted in 1973. The second was called the Report on "National Judicature: Equal Justice—Social Justice". The Committee was chaired by Justice P.N. Bhagwati and the report was submitted during the Emergency. Both reports emphasised the role of the 'panchayats', manned by people with the knowledge of local custom, in removing the defects of the British system of justice administration.

Box 5.6: Emergence of Public Interest Litigation (PIL)

- Populism during Emergency: Report of the Krishna Iyer Committee and of the Bhagwati Committee—insertion of Article 39A by the Forty-Second Amendment, 1976.
- Judicial Populism: The sensitivity of judges and lawyers to exploitation and suffering, and consequent judicial activism—it was partly an attempt to clean the image of the judiciary tarnished by many decisions during the Emergency—thus, PIL became a judge-led and judge-induced phenomenon.
- Post-Emergency Press, anxious to expose Government repression and exploitative social structures, helped activists and groups bring in national limelight major as well as minor instances of injustice.
- The verdict in the First Judges Case, 1981, expanded the locus standi or 'standing' in the court—this ultimately helped the practice of filing cases by anyone in the 'public interest', i.e. PIL.
- In the Bandhua Mukti Morcha (BMM) case, 1984, the SC bench of Justices P.N. Bhagwati, R.S. Pathak, A.S. Sen famously converted a complaint letter into a petition.

Evaluation of Public Interest Litigation (PIL)

PIL was primarily an innovation in legal procedure. Its defining features emerged in the early years.[47]

Box 5.7: Features of the PIL

- Relaxed rules of locus standi.
- Simplified formal requirements regarding the lodging of a petition.
- Evidence gathering by a commission appointed by the court, the procedure of which is claimed to be 'non-adversarial'.
- The court can order far-reaching remedial measures, the execution of which is supervised and followed up by the court.

It was the activism of the many judges driven by socialist ideology and egalitarian values that led to the evolution of PIL, eventually leading to the emergence of 'activist' judiciary. Through the tool of PIL, the judiciary expanded its role in governance—amounting to 'judicialization' of governance. As a result, the judiciary has become more "embedded" as a political actor.[48] Over four decades of the practice of PIL has resulted in many significant administrative interventions by the judiciary in various areas of public policy.[49]

Box 5.8: Judicialization of Governance—Some Instances

- Environmental policy—the judiciary appointed special investigatory or monitoring committees.
- Corruption—in order to avoid political interference with investigation, the judiciary ordered CBI, ED, etc., to directly report to the Court.
- Affirmative Action/Reservation Policy—judiciary developed the concept of creamy layer.

The practice of PIL has undergone many changes over the period.[50] Firstly, in the initial period, behind each PIL petitioner the judiciary could see a specific group of people in urgent need of justice. In more recent period, PILs are filed on issues affecting general citizenry, rather than on behalf of individual victims of injustice. Secondly, since the mid-1990's, the judiciary began to appoint amicus curiae, many times replacing the initial applicants. It is observed that public- spirited petitioners "now often appear as impediments to justice rather than its allies." Thirdly, the instances of *'suo moto'* cases, i.e. the judiciary taking cognisance of a case on its own, have increased.

Judicial activism and judicialization of governance have crossed all limits and in the end, have ended in making the judiciary more powerful. Former CJI Hidayatullah had reportedly predicted in 1984 that PIL will result in annihilation of all procedure.[51] But it has resulted in much more. Justice Markandey Katju had warned, delivering a judgement in 2006, that if "there is a law, judges can certainly enforce it, but judges cannot create a law and seek to enforce it. Judges must know their limits and must not try to run the government. ... There is a broad separation of powers under the Constitution and no organ of the State ... should encroach into each other's domain. ... we are repeatedly coming across cases where judges are unjustifiably trying to perform executive or legislative functions."[52]

Legal expert Rajeev Dhavan, however, counters Justice Katju. He contends that there is a difference between "judicial activism"—which according to Dhavan is permissible; and "judicial excessivism"—which according to him, is not. Dhavan feels that "India has a forward- looking activist Constitution to impart human rights and social justice for all. Judges cannot shy away from fulfilling this dream for all people by inventing new legal techniques to ensure it."[53] It must be said, however, that PIL has indeed led to judicial excessivism; has challenged the principle of checks and balance; and has empowered the judiciary beyond imagination of the framers of the Constitution.

QUESTIONS

Write Short Answers (5 marks each):

1. Explain the terms 'higher judiciary' and 'subordinate judiciary'.
2. What are the constitutional provisions regarding the appointment of judges in the subordinate judiciary?
3. How does the Constitution secure judicial independence?
4. Explain the procedure of appointment of SC and HC judges as laid down in Articles 124 and 216 respectively.
5. Describe the procedure to impeach a Supreme Court judge.
6. Describe the composition of the National Judicial Appointments Commission under the now-invalidated Ninety-Ninth Amendment.

Answer the Following (15 marks each):

1. Explain the significance of 'separation of powers' and 'checks and balance' in securing judicial independence.
2. What is the power to judicial review? Trace the evolution of judicial review in India.
3. Examine the causes of and cases leading to the emergence of Collegium System of appointment of SC and HC judges.
4. What is Public Interest Litigation? How is it different from normal litigation? What were the causes and events responsible for development of PIL in India?
5. Do you think PIL represents judicial excessivism leading to judicialization of governance? Give reasons.

PROJECT SUGGESTIONS

1. Conduct a debate/discussion in the class on "Collegium System vs NJAC".
2. Prepare a PPT presentation on "Collegium System, PIL and checks and balance".

ENDNOTES

1. See Article 233: Appointment of district judges - Constitution of India.
2. See Article 234: Recruitment of persons other than district judges to the judicial service - Constitution of India.
3. See Article 130: Seat of Supreme Court - Constitution of India.
4. See Article 124: Establishment and constitution of Supreme Court - Constitution of India.
5. See for concerned Articles Part V Archives - Constitution of India.
6. See Article 214: High Courts for States - Constitution of India.
7. See Article 230: Extension of jurisdiction of High Courts to Union territories - Constitution of India.
8. See Article 231: Establishment of a common High Court for two or more States - Constitution of India.
9. For Articles 216 to 222, see Part VI Archives - Constitution of India.
10. See Article 145: Rules of Court, etc. - Constitution of India.
11. For Article 146, see Article 146: Officers and servants and the expenses of the Supreme Court - Constitution of India and for Article 229, see Article 229: Officers and servants and the expenses of High Courts - Constitution of India.
12. See Article 227: Power of superintendence over all courts by the High Court - Constitution of India.
13. Ambedkar, *CAD, 8-90-157* 24 May 1949 Archives - Constitution of India.
14. Sajjan Singh vs State of Rajasthan.
15. I. C. Golaknath & Ors vs State of Punjab & Anrs. (With Connected ... on 27 February, 1967.
16. Bank Nationalisation case Rustom Cavasjee Cooper vs Union of India on 10 February, 1970 ; Privy Purses case H. H. Maharajadhiraja Madhav Rao Jiwaji ... vs Union of India on 15 December, 1970.
17. Twenty-Fourth Amendment, The Constitution (Twenty-fourth Amendment) Act, 1971, National Portal of India ; Twenty-Fifth Amendment, The Constitution (Twenty-fifth Amendment) Act, 1971, National Portal of India.
18. Kesavananda Bharati Sripadagalvaru ... vs State of Kerala and Anr on 24 April, 1973 (indiankanoon.org).
19. CJI S.M. Sikri and Justices K.S. Hegde, Mukherjea, J.M. Shelat, A.N. Grover, Jaganmohan Reddy and H.R. Khanna formed the majority opinion; whereas Justices A.N. Ray, D.G. Palekar, K.K. Mathew, M.H. Beg, S.N. Dwivedi and Y.V. Chandrachud formed the minority opinion.
20. Indira Nehru Gandhi vs Shri Raj Narain & Anr on 7 November, 1975.

21. Indira Nehru Gandhi vs Shri Raj Narain & Anr on 7 November, 1975.
22. Waman Rao & Ors. etc. vs Union of India and Ors on 9 May, 1980.
23. *CAD 8-90-15 24 May 1949 Archives - Constitution of India.*
24. *CAD 8-90-28, ibid.*
25. *CAD 8-90-53, ibid.*
26. *CAD 8-90-157, ibid.*
27. *CAD 8-90-158, ibid.*
28. For details, see Granville Austin *Working a Democratic Constitution* (1999, OUP) Chapter 5.
29. *Ibid* Chapter 12; also see Dhananjay Mahapatra "Appointments of CJIs through supersessions", *The Times of India* 29 June 2020 Appointment of CJIs through supersessions, a sin never repeated after period of Emergency, India News - Times of India.
30. Mahapatra, *ibid.*
31. *ibid.*
32. See Austin *op cit.*
33. See Austin *op cit.*
34. J.R. Gagrat, *An examination of the executive tools used to influence judicial appointments to the Supreme court of india and the High courts in the context of the Indian Emergency (1975-77),* a Thesis submitted for MA to Cornell University, 2019, pp 45–48. Available on content.
35. Austin, *op cit,* p 288.
36. Austin, *op cit,* p 288.
37. For details, see Vansh Bhatnagar, *Jus Corpus Law Journal*, Vol. 2, issue 1, September–November 2021 CollegiumSystem-Bhatnagar.pdf ; see also Fahad Nahvi & Yagnesh Sharma, "The Collegium vs the NJAC" Social Policy Research Foundation Discussion Paper, 4 July 2023, The Collegium vs The NJAC: Navigating Judicial Independence ; Law Bhoomi Collegium System vs NJAC in India.
38. See Bhatnagar *ibid;* Nahvi and Sharma *ibid.*
39. A report by Anurakti Sharma in *Times Now,* 20 January 2023, Ignoring R&AW objections, SC sends gay judge Kirpal's name for HC judges again, India News, Times Now.
40. Nahvi & Sharma, *op cit.*
41. See 4042gi.p65.
42. Justices J.H. Khehar, J. Chelameswar, M.B. Lokur, Kurian Joseph and A.K. Goel formed the bench. Justice Chelameswar was the lone dissenting judge. See Supreme Court Advocates-on-Record ... vs Union of India on 16 October, 2015.
43. For details, see Bhatnagar, *op cit.*

44. Manoj Mate "Two Paths to Judicial Power: The Basic Structure Doctrine and Public Interest Litigation in Comparative Perspective" *San Diego International Law Journal*, Vol. 12, 2010 , p 195, Microsoft Word - Mate.
45. Upendra Baxi "Taking Suffering Seriously: Social Action Litigation in the Supreme Court of India", *Third World Legal Studies*, Vol. 4, Article 6, 1985, pp 111–116 Taking Suffering Seriously: Social Action Litigation in the Supreme Court of India.
46. Anuj Bhuwania, "Courting the People: The Rise of Public Interest Litigation in Post-Emergency India" *Comparative Studies of South Asia, Africa and the Middle East*, Vol. 34 no 2, 2014, p 325 cssaame_article_published-libre.pdf.
47. Bhuwania *ibid* p 327.
48. Mate *op cit* p 214.
49. Mate *ibid* pp 202–209.
50. For details, see Bhuwania *op cit* pp 330–333.
51. Quoted by Bhuwania *ibid* p 333.
52. Quoted by Mate *op cit* p 177.
53. Quoted by Mate *ibid* p 221.

6

Election Commission and Elections

Elections are the single most important instrument that helps materialise the idea of rule by the people. Conduct of the elections is of paramount importance in a democracy, as it helps people to express their will through their vote and leads to the formation of a government that a majority wishes. It was *extremely* important, thus, for India to ensure that all elections will be conducted in a free and fair manner. It adopted an autonomous machinery with a constitutional status for the purposes, namely the Election Commission. Provisions regarding the Election Commission as well as conduct of elections are mentioned in the Constitution and further supported by laws passed by the Parliament.

6.1 CONSTITUENT ASSEMBLY DEBATES

The provisions regarding the Election Commission were debated in detail in the Constituent Assembly. However, there was no much debate over another important aspect of the electoral process, viz. franchise, who gets the right to vote. It appears that there was near unanimity over introducing the universal adult franchise, i.e. the right to vote for every adult citizen of India.

Universal Adult Franchise

The Nehru Report, 1928 envisaged the lower house of Parliament to be elected by all adults.[1] Karachi Resolution 1931, of Indian National Congress included universal adult suffrage as part of the Fundamental Rights.[2] Thus, a right to vote to all adults was already on the agenda of the Constituent Assembly. The Draft Constitution of 1948 (DC-1948) adopted adult suffrage for the election of the House of the People as well as State Assemblies.[3] Property holding or tax payment were never thought to be the criteria for being a voter. As explained in Chapter 1, all elections conducted during the colonial period, including the election to the Constituent Assembly were held on these criteria.

Some members of the Constituent Assembly, however, expressed concern over introducing adult suffrage. These were primarily on the ground of extensive illiteracy among Indians existing at the time of independence. K.T. Shah, while moving an amendment to the qualifications for contesting election, said that the condition of literacy can be made at least for the candidates seeking election.[4] H.N. Kunzru thought it would be wiser to bring adult franchise in an incremental way.[5] However, as noted, the demand for universal adult franchise preceded the formation of the Constituent Assembly, and the Assembly had no difficulty in adopting the same.

Election Commission

Provisions regarding the composition and functioning of the Election Commission went through several iterations, from the DC-1948 to the final version included in the Constitution. The DC-1948 provided for two separate authorities to conduct federal and state elections.[6] However, during the session of the Constituent Assembly held on 15 June 1949, B.R. Ambedkar presented an amendment to the provisions in the DC-1948, that suggested a single Commission to be appointed by the President for conducting federal and state elections.[7]

This amendment was discussed extensively in the Constituent Assembly, in a debate touching upon various aspects of the issue, and in which several members participated.[8] There were two main issues on which the members argued. One, the desirability of a single commission; and two, the wisdom of the President appointing the Commissioners and making rules governing their service.

As regards the first issue, from two sets of election commissions to having only one election commission and a centralised election process was a "radical change'', agreed Ambedkar. He contended that the change was necessitated by observations brought to the notice of the Drafting Committee (DC), that governments in states with diverse populations are working towards denying enrolment in voters' list to the minority population.[9] Among the members, H.V. Pataskar made the most scathing criticism of this argument. After detailing the flip-flop from one commission to separate commissions for federal and state elections, and back to a single commission, Pataskar questioned all arguments made in favour of a single commission. He went on to argue, "To my mind the reason for all these changes is to be found in the fact that we are now trying gradually to move away from the idea of federation."[10] Shibban Lal Saxena introduced an extensive amendment to the Amendment moved by Ambedkar. It gave a larger role to the Parliament in making conditions of service and appointment of the commission.[11] After a prolonged debate, the provisions regarding the electoral process took shape as reflected in the Constitution.

TABLE 6.1 Provisions in the Draft Constitution and Amendments Moved

Provisions of the Draft Constitution of 1948	*Amendments suggested by B.R. Ambedkar in the Constituent Assembly*	*Amendments suggested by Shibban Lal Saxena to Ambedkar's Amendments in the Constituent Assembly*
Two separate commissions, one in the centre and one in each state. The commission in the centre to conduct elections to the Parliament, and of President and Vice President; to be appointed by the President. The commission in the States to conduct elections to the State Legislature and of Governor; to be appointed by the Governor.	Single commission to conduct elections to the Parliament, the State Legislatures and of the President and the Vice President; to be appointed by the President. Provision to appoint Regional Commissioners (RCs) by the President, if he thinks necessary. Conditions of service of CEC, ECs and RCs to be determined by a rule made by the President. The CEC shall not be removed except in the manner of a judge of the Supreme Court; other commissioners shall not be removed except on recommendation of the CEC.	Single commission; but, appointment of the election commissioners by the President to be confirmed by 2/3 majority in joint session of the Parliament. The conditions of their service to be determined by a law of the Parliament.

6.2 CONSTITUTIONAL PROVISIONS REGARDING ELECTION COMMISSION

Provisions regarding Elections are included in Part XV of the Constitution, in Articles 324 to 329.[12] The Constitution gave the power to appoint the CEC and the ECs, "subject to the provision of a law made by the Parliament for the purpose." But making such a law was not interpreted to be mandatory until recently. The Act passed by the Parliament in 1991 (see below) too did not provide for qualifications or provision of appointment of the CEC and ECs. These were finally made by the Act of the Parliament in December 2023.

TABLE 6.2 Constitutional Provisions

Article	*Provisions Regarding Elections*
324 (1)	Provides for an Election Commission to superintend, direct and control the elections to both Houses of the Parliament, the State Legislatures, as well as the election of the President and the Vice President.
324 (2)	Stipulates that the Election Commission will have one Chief Election Commissioner (CEC); and it will also have more such Election Commissioners (EC) if the President so desires. It further stipulates that the President will appoint the CEC and the ECs, subject to the provision of a law made by the Parliament for the purpose.
324 (3)	In case of a multi-member Election Commission, the CEC acts as the Chairperson.
324 (4)	Confers upon the President the power to appoint, in consultation with the Election Commission, any Regional Commissioners, if required.
324 (5)	Provides that the condition of service and tenure of the CEC, ECs and Regional Commissioners will be determined by President, subject to the provisions of any law made by the Parliament. It further says that the CEC will not be removed from the office except in the manner as the judge of the Supreme Court; and the ECs and Regional Commissioners will not be removed except on the recommendation by the CEC.
325	Makes provision for a single electoral roll for both parliamentary and legislative elections. It categorically says that no person will be ineligible for inclusion in such roll, on grounds of religion, race, caste or sex.
326	Says that elections to the lower house of the Parliament and to the lower house of the state legislatures will be on the basis of adult suffrage. The eligibility age for voting was 21 until 1988; when it was brought down to 18 by the Constitution (Sixty-first Amendment Act), 1988.
327	Confers the power to make provisions about all matters relating to elections to the Parliament and State Legislature—such as preparation of electoral rolls, delimitation of constituencies, etc.—on the Parliament of India.
328	Confers upon the State Legislatures the power to make provisions regarding election to the Legislature of the State, unless the Parliament has made a law regarding such matter.
329	Stipulates that no law relating to the delimitation of constituencies and allotment of seats to such constituencies shall be questioned in any court. It further stipulates that no election to the Parliament of State Legislature shall be questioned except by an election petition presented to an authority as prescribed by law.

The Thirty-Ninth Amendment (1975) passed during the Emergency inserted Article 329A in Chapter XV.[13] This Article exempted the Prime Minister and the Speaker from any cases regarding their election to the Lok Sabha. The Amendment was a response to the decision of the Allahabad HC, invalidating the election of Indira Gandhi to Lok Sabha. This Article was later deleted by the Forty-Fourth Amendment (1978).

6.3 EVOLUTION OF THE ELECTION COMMISSION

Single Member Election Commission

The Parliament was expected to make a law laying down the conditions for appointment and service of the CEC and ECs, which was made in 1991. For over four decades after the promulgation of the Constitution, the Election Commission had only one member, the CEC; appointed by the President (as per Article 74(1), by the government of the day) under Article 324 (2). During this period, nine General elections—first eight and the tenth—were conducted by single-member Commissions; while only one—the ninth—was conducted by a three-member Commission. In the absence of any specific law determining the conditions of service, the CECs enjoyed varied terms of office. Some of them went on to hold other important offices in the Government after demitting the office of the CEC. Despite no such qualification being laid down by the Constitution or subsequently, the law, all CECs and ECs so far have been selected from the civil services/bureaucracy.

TABLE 6.3 Chief Election Commissioners—1950–1990

	Name	*Tenure*[14]	*No. of Parliamentary Elections Conducted*	*After demitting Office of CEC*
1	Sukumar Sen	20/03/1950–19/12/1958 8 years and 9 months	2	Appointed First Vice Chancellor of Burdwan University in 1960.
2	K.V.K Sundaram	20/12/1958–30/09/1967 8 years and 9 months	2	Appointed Chairperson of the Fifth Law Commission in 1968.
3	S.P. Sen Verma	01/10/1967–30/09/1972 5 years	1	
4	Nagendra Singh	01/10/1972–06/02/1973 4 months and 6 days	None	Appointed India's Representative to the International Court of Justice.

(Contd.)

	Name	*Tenure*[14]	*No. of Parliamentary Elections Conducted*	*After demitting Office of CEC*
5	T. Swaminathan	07/02/1973–17/06/1977 4 years and 4 months	1	
6	S.L. Shakdhar	18/06/1977–17/06/1982 5 years	1	
7	R.K. Trivedi	18/06/1982–31/12/1985 3 years and 6 months	1	Appointed Governor of Gujarat in 1986.
8	R.V.S. Peri Sastri	01/01/1986–25/11/1990 4 years and 11 months	1	
9	V.S. Ramadevi	26/11/1990–11/12/1990 16 days	None	Secretary General of Rajya Sabha, 1993–1997; Governor of Karnataka, 1999–2002.

Period of Transition

For the first time in the history of the Election Commission, President Venkataraman appointed two additional ECs, S.S. Dhanoa and V.S. Seigell on 16 October 1989. The differences between the Rajiv Gandhi Government and the then CEC R.V.S. Peri Sastri was widely perceived as the reason for the same.[15] The discord between the Government and the CEC became apparent again the very next day, when the Government made public its decision to hold the elections on 22 November. Not only was the CEC not consulted before doing so, but the Government also deprived him of the prerogative to announce the dates of elections.[16] The ninth General election was conducted by a three-member Commission.

After being elected to power, the V.P. Singh Government decided to revert to single-member Commission and terminated the services of two additional ECs from 2 January 1990.[17] However, S.S. Dhanoa, one of the two ECs whose services were thus terminated, went to the Supreme Court against this order. The Supreme Court pointed out the Constitutional provision that the CEC is placed on par with the Supreme Court judge in terms of removal from office; but the same is not the case for the other ECs. They could be removed by the President on the recommendation of the CEC.[18] Thus, his petition was dismissed in July 1991.

The V.P. Singh Government did not last long and Chandrashekhar assumed charge as Prime Minister on 10 Nov 1990. His government appointed V.S. Ramadevi as the CEC on 26 Nov 1990. She was the first, and so far the only, woman to become the CEC.[19] For reasons quite unclear so far, she was replaced within just 16 days, and the Chandrashekhar Government appointed T.N. Seshan as CEC on 12 Dec 1990.[20] His Government passed the much-awaited law—the Election Commission (Conditions of Service of Election Commissioners and Transaction of Business) Act—on 25 January 1991.[21] This law fixed the term of office of the CEC and the ECs at 6 years or 65 years of age, whichever is earlier. It also determined the salary, pension, etc. for the CEC and the ECs. The law did not, however, change the mode of appointment of the CEC and the ECs. They continued to be appointed by the President (by implication by the government of the day) under Article 324 (2) of the Constitution.

Shift to Three-Member Election Commission

Between January 1990 and September 1993, the Commission remained single-member. T.N. Seshan conducted the tenth General election in May-June 1991 (which became necessary after the fall of the Chandrashekhar Government in March 1991) as the single-member Commission. Later, however, the P.V. Narasimha Rao Government as well as the opposition parties were becoming increasingly unhappy with the style of functioning of T.N. Seshan. Thus, in a sudden, unexpected move, the Government appointed two additional ECs on 1 October 1993. The two new ECs were G.V.G. Krishnamurthy and M.S. Gill.[22] Further, the Government introduced an Ordinance (that later became Chapter III of the Law of 1991), which stated that the decisions be taken by consensus "as far as possible"; and in case of disagreements within members, the decision be taken by majority.[23] This rule brought about parity of status of the CEC and the ECs in terms of the functioning of the Commission. Three-member election commission became a norm after 1993. However, the CECs and ECs continued to be appointed by the President (again, by implication by the government of the day) under Article 324 (2) of the Constitution. There was no change in the way the CEC and ECs were appointed.

A writ petition was filed in the Supreme Court of India in 2015 regarding the appointment of the CEC and the ECs. Three more writ petitions were filed subsequently in 2017, 2021 and 2022. Bunching all these petitions, the Supreme Court delivered its judgement on 2 March 2023. It called for the appointment of the CEC and the ECs by the President on the advice of a committee consisting of the Prime Minister of India, the Leader of the Opposition in the Lok Sabha and the Chief Justice of India. It added, "This norm will continue to hold good till a law is made by the Parliament."[24]

As per the directions of the Supreme Court, a bill was introduced in the Parliament in August 2023, and subsequently passed in December 2023. This Act, called the "The Chief Election Commissioner and Other Election

Commissioners (Appointment, Conditions of Service and Term of Office) Act 2023" replaced 1991 Act regarding the conditions of service and term of office of the CEC and ECs.[25] This law, for the first time, set the qualifications for the CEC and the ECs—a person holding or having held the rank of a Secretary to the Government of India or a post equivalent to that. It provides for a search committee headed by the Law Minister and consisting of two other members not below the rank of a Secretary; to prepare a panel of five persons. The committee consisting of the Prime Minister of India, the Leader of the Opposition in the Lok Sabha and a Union Cabinet Minister to be appointed by the Prime Minister of India will then select one name and recommend the same to the President for appointment.

Meanwhile, a controversy erupted just at a time when the announcement of the dates of the eighteenth General election was due. EC Arun Goel tendered his resignation suddenly on 9 March 2024.[26] Another EC, Anupchandra Pande, had retired in February 2024. Thus, the Commission was reduced to only the CEC. While under the Constitution and the new law, it is possible to hold elections only with one member (CEC), the Government of Prime Minister Modi decided to appoint two ECs under the new law. Thus, Gyanesh Kumar and Sukhbir Sandhu were appointed ECs before the announcement of General election.

Unlike their predecessors, the CECs and ECs appointed since the 1990's have rarely been given important positions by the Government after retirement. However, there are a few exceptions. After his retirement in 2001, M.S. Gill joined the Indian National Congress. He was given a ticket to Rajya Sabha in 2004, and was elected for two consecutive terms. He also served as a Minister in the Government of Prime Minister Manmohan Singh from 2009 until 2011.[27] T.N. Seshan, after retiring as the CEC in December 1996, contested the election for President as an independent in July 1997. He lost the election to K.R. Narayanan, the candidate of the Congress party. Later, during the 1999 Lok Sabha election, the Congress party gave ticket to Seshan to contest against Lal Krishna Advani from Gandhinagar, Gujarat. Seshan lost this election too.[28] Recently, Sushil Chandra, who retired as CEC in May 2022, was appointed as a non-judicial member of the Lokpal in February 2024.[29]

Box 6.1: Points to Remember

- The previous norm of single-member commission as well as the current norm of three-member commission, were both a product of political convenience, particularly that of the ruling dispensation of the day.
- No government found it essential, nor convenient, to change the procedure of appointment of the CEC and the ECs prescribed in the Constitution, until an intervention by the Supreme Court while giving judgements on public interest litigation, in 2023.
- Many CECs appointed until the 1990's have enjoyed another office of importance under the Government, after demitting the office of CEC. However, those appointed after the 1990's—with a few exceptions—have rarely enjoyed this benefit.

6.4 CONDUCT OF ELECTIONS

As stated above, while the Constitution has vested the power to superintend, direct and control the elections in the Election Commission, it has conferred the power to make provisions about all matters relating to elections on the Parliament. Thus, the Representation of People Act was passed in 1951. It is an extensive law governing almost all aspects related to elections. The law has been amended several times to bring about more accountability and transparency.

Delimitation

Elections to the Lok Sabha and the State Legislative Assemblies are conducted in single member territorial constituencies on the basis of the first past the pole system. Delimitation means the process of drawing of boundaries of such territorial constituencies. Under Article 82 of the Constitution, Parliament makes law from time to time to create a Delimitation Commission from time to time to undertake this exercise.[30] The orders of the Delimitation Commission have the force of law. They are sent to both Houses of Parliament and State Legislatures, but they cannot modify the orders. And the orders of the Delimitation Commission cannot be questioned in any court. Its orders come into effect on a date specified by the President. So far, four Delimitation Commissions were created by the Act of the Parliament, in 1952, 1962 and 1972 and 2002.[31]

TABLE 6.4 Provisions of Representation of People Act 1951[32]
(Note: Part VIII of the Act was omitted by an amendment made in 1966)

Part of the Act	*Provisions*
Part I	Short title and interpretation.
Part II	Qualifications and Disqualifications: Separate chapters dealing with qualifications for membership of the Parliament and State Legislatures; disqualifications for membership of the Parliament and State Legislatures; and disqualifications for voting.
Part III	Notification of General Elections—to be issued on the recommendation of Election Commission.
Part IV	Administrative machinery for the conduct of elections.
Part IV A	Registration of Political Parties.
Part V	Conduct of elections: provisions regarding nomination of candidates, agents of the candidates, general procedure, poll, counting of votes, declaration of assets and liabilities, election expenses.
Part V A	Free supply of certain material to candidates of recognised political parties.

(Contd.)

Part of the Act	Provisions
Part VI	Disputes regarding elections: trial and withdrawal of election petitions, appeal.
Part VII	Corrupt practices and electoral offences.
Part IX	Bye-elections
Part X	Miscellaneous
Part XI	General

TABLE 6.5 Major Amendments to Representation of People Act 1951[33]

Amendment Year	Provisions
1966	Election Tribunals were abolished upon the recommendation of the Election Commission—provision to refer the cases related to elections directly to the High Courts.
1989	Provision for adjournment or countermanding of elections inserted in case of booth capturing—it also made provision for registration of political parties—it further provided legal basis for introduction of voting machines.
1996	Empowered the Election Commission to appoint Observers in constituencies during elections—included provision to list the names of the candidates in alphabetical order on the ballot paper/voting machine.
2002	A new section 33A was inserted to protect the right to information of the voters—this mandated the filing of an affidavit by all candidates on their background.
2010	Made provisions for the voting rights of non-resident Indians.
2013	The amendment, passed to obviate a 2013 judgement of the Supreme Court, provided that a person can contest election even if he/she is in police custody or jail—it further provided that disqualification to contest or of a member will be only after conviction for specified offence.

Initiatives by the Election Commission

The Election Commission cannot make laws governing the electoral process. However, it has contributed in its own ways to improve the conduct of elections.[34] The most well-known among these are the introduction of EVMs and the VVPAT. The Commission has also diligently worked towards implementation of the model code of conduct during elections, despite the fact that it does not have the backing of a law. In recent years, the Commission has worked proactively to improve voter awareness and participation.

Box 6.2: Initiatives Taken by the Election Commission

- Model Code of Conduct: rules to be followed by political parties and candidates during elections—implemented by the Election Commission—do not have statutory backing.
- Electronic Voting Machines (EVMs): first conceived by the Election Commission in 1977—after a long process of development and trials, used in Assembly elections since 2001—used in Lok Sabha elections since 2004.
- Voter Verified Paper Audit Trail (VVPAT): suggested by some political parties in 2010 for promoting further transparency and verifiability in poll process.
- Systematic Voters' Education and Electoral Participation (SVEEP): the flagship programme of the Election Commission for voter education, spreading voter awareness and promoting voter literacy.

Elections in India

The Election Commission has successfully conducted eighteen elections to Lok Sabha, several elections to State Legislative Assemblies, besides conducting periodic elections to Rajya Sabha and for the offices of the President and the Vice President of India. Conduct of Lok Sabha election is a massive exercise. Below is a summary of Lok Sabha elections in India.

TABLE 6.6 Lok Sabha Elections in a Nutshell

Election/ Year, CEC (SM/MM)	*Duration/ Dates*	*Turnout %*	*Majority Party/Largest Party (Seats/Vote %)*	*Second Largest Party (Seats/Vote %)*
I – 1952 **(ONOE)** Sukumar Sen (SM)	2 days 25 Oct 51 & 21 Feb 52	44.87	Indian National Congress (Congress) (364/44.99)	Socialist Party (12/10.59)
II – 1957 **(ONOE)** Sukumar Sen (SM)	2 days 27 Feb, 9 Jun 57	45.44	Congress (371/47.78)	Praja Socialist Party (19/10.41)
III – 1962 **(ONOE)** K.V.K. Sundaram (SM)	2 days 19, 25 Feb 62	55.42	Congress (361/44.72)	Communist Party of India (29/9.94)

(Contd.)

Election/ Year, CEC (SM/MM)	*Duration/ Dates*	*Turnout %*	*Majority Party/Largest Party (Seats/Vote %)*	*Second Largest Party (Seats/Vote %)*
IV – 1967 **(ONOE)** K.V.K. Sundaram (SM)	2 days 17, 21 Feb 67	61.04	Congress (283/40.78)	Swatantra Party (44/8.67)
V – 1971 S.P. Sen Verma (SM)	2 days 1, 10 Mar 71	55.27	Congress (352/43.68)	Communist Party of India (Marxist) (25/5.12)
VI – 1977 T. Swaminathan (SM)	2 days 16, 20 Mar 77	60.49	Janata Party (295/41.32)	Congress (154/34.52)
VII – 1980 S.L. Shakdhar (SM)	2 days 3, 6 Jan 80	59.92	Congress (353/42.69)	Janata Party (Secular) (41/9.39)
VIII –1984 R.K. Trivedi (SM)	3 days 24, 27, 28 Dec 84	64.01	Congress (404/49.10)	Telugu Desam Party (30/4.31)
IX – 1989 R.V.S. Peri Sastri (MM)	2 days 22, 26 Nov 89	61.95	Congress (197/39.53)	Janata Dal (143/17.79)
X – 1991 T.N. Seshan (SM)	3 days 20 May, 12, 15 Jun 91	56.73	Congress (232/36.26)	Bharatiya Janata Party (BJP) (120/20.11)
XI – 1996 T.N. Seshan (MM)	3 days 27 Apr, 2, 7 May 96	57.94	BJP (161/20.29)	Congress (140/28.80)
XII – 1998 M.S. Gill (MM)	3 days 16, 22, 28 Feb 98	61.97	BJP (182/25.59)	Congress (141/25.82)
XIII – 1999 M.S. Gill (MM)	5 days 4 Sep – 1 Oct 99	59.99	BJP (182/23.75)	Congress (114/28.30)
XIV – 2004 T. S. Krishna Murthy (MM)	4 days 28 Apr – 10 May 04	58.07	Congress (145/26.53)	BJP (138/22.16)

(Contd.)

Election/ Year, CEC (SM/MM)	*Duration/ Dates*	*Turnout %*	*Majority Party/Largest Party (Seats/Vote %)*	*Second Largest Party (Seats/Vote %)*
XV – 2009 N. Gopalaswami, Navin Chawla (MM)	5 days 16 Apr – 13 May 09	58.21	Congress (206/20.55)	BJP (116/18.80)
XVI – 2014 V.S. Sampath (MM)	10 days 7 Apr – 12 May 14	66.44	BJP (282/31)	Congress (44/19.31)
XVII – 2019 Sunil Arora (MM)	7 days 11 Apr – 19 May 19	67.40	BJP (303/37.30)	Congress (52/19.46)
XVIII – 2024 Rajiv Kumar (MM)	7 days 19 Apr – 1 June 24	66.33	BJP (240/36.56)	Congress (99/21.96)

(**Note:** ONOE = One Nation One Election)

SUGGESTIONS FOR CLASSROOM DISCUSSIONS/ASSIGNMENTS

In the Classroom: Understand the election process, the polling administration by reading the relevant sections of Representation of People Act 1951;

Debate the Electoral Bonds and election funding.

Assignments: Compare India's introduction of adult franchise with that in other countries;

(a) Find out information about conduct of elections in other major democracies and compare the process with that in India;

(b) Evaluate the implementation of Model Code of Conduct and challenges to it

(c) Teachers can motivate to read the text of the provisions in the Constitution as well as that of the Law.

QUESTIONS

Write Short Answers (5 marks each):

1. What is the importance of Election Commission of India?
2. Comment briefly on introducing universal adult franchise in the Constitution.
3. What is delimitation? How is it conducted?

Answer the Following (15 marks each):

1. What factors led to the transition from a single-member Election Commission to a multi-member one?
2. Write a note on the initiatives taken by the Election Commission towards making elections more inclusive and accessible.
3. Evaluate the impact of the Acts of 1991 and 2023 on the appointment of the Election Commission.

PROJECT SUGGESTIONS

1. Conduct a competition in class to create Political Satire Through Art-Design, humorous yet informative memes about elections and political campaigns. Focus on ethics, fake promises, and election gimmicks.
2. Make a PPT presentation on arguments over the forthcoming delimitation. Focus on the arguments of the Southern States, of the need to increase the number of representatives.
3. Conduct a debate/discussion in the class on "Whether to go back to paper ballot or to continue with EVMs".

ENDNOTES

1. *Nehru Report* 10, Nehru Report (Motilal Nehru,1928) Archives - Constitution of India.
2. *Karachi Resolution,* 1931, Karachi Resolution 1931 (Jawaharlal Nehru) Archives - Constitution of India.
3. *Draft Constitution of India, 1948 (DCI,1948),* Draft Constitution of India 1948 Archives - Constitution of India.
4. *CAD* 8-97-168, 02 Jun 1949 Archives - Constitution of India.
5. *CAD,* 11-162-74, 22 Nov 1949 Archives - Constitution of India.
6. Draft Constitution, Part XIII, Elections, Articles 289, 290, 291, *DCI, 1948, op cit.*
7. *CAD,* 8.105.204, 15 Jun 1949 Archives - Constitution of India.
8. For complete speeches of all members who participated in this debate, see debates on 15 and 16 June 2024, from 8.105.205 to 8.105.237, *CAD, ibid; a*nd from 8.106.4 to 8.106.45, and *CAD* 16 Jun 1949 Archives - Constitution of India.
9. *CAD,* 8.105.212, 15 Jun 1949 Archives - Constitution of India.
10. *CAD,* 8.105.237, *ibid.*
11. *CAD,* 8.105.219, *ibid.*
12. Part XV Archives - Constitution of India.
13. Article 329A in Constitution of India.
14. *Election Commission* eci.gov.in/former-cec-ec.
15. Inder Jit, "Poll Body, pressures and independence" *Arunachal Times,* 20 November 2022 Poll body, pressures & independence, The Arunachal Times.
16. Dolly Chingakham, "Selection of election commissioners on advice of panel of PM, LoP, CJI: All about poll body appointments" *India Today,* 02 March 2023, Selection of election commissioners on advice of panel of PM, LoP, CJI: All about poll body appointments - India Today.
17. Dolly Chingakham *ibid.*
18. N.S. Babitha "Certainty of the tenure of the Election Commissioners: a paramount need" *ILI Law Review,* vol II, winter 2019 nsb.pdf (ili.ac.in)
19. *Election Commission, op cit.*
20. *Election Commission, op cit.*
21. *Indian Kanoon* Election Commission (Conditions of Service of Election Commissioners and Transaction of Business) Act, 1991 (indiankanoon.org).
22. Manoj Mitta, "With two more election commissioners, T.N. Seshan's wings likely to be clipped" *India Today,* 31 October 1993. It takes three to tango - India Today.
23. *Ibid;* for details of the provisions in the law, also see *Indian Kanoon, op.cit.*

24. *Supreme Court of India,* 1458_2015_3_1501_42634_Judgement_02-Mar-2023.pdf (sci.gov.in).

25. *National Informatics Centre,* a2023-49.pdf (indiacode.nic.in).

26. Soni Mishra, "Arun Goel Resignation: Rumours suggest discord with CEC led to surprise move" *The Week,* 10 March 2024. Arun Goel resignation: Rumours suggest discord with CEC led to surprise move - The Week.

27. "Former poll panel chief and Congress leader MS Gill dies at 86" *India Today,* 15 October 2023. Former poll panel chief and Congress leader MS Gill dies at 86 - India Today accessed on.

28. "When Shiv Sena backed T.N. Seshan for President in 1997" *The Week.* When Shiv Sena backed T.N. Seshan for president in 1997 - The Week.

29. *Lokpal* LOKPAL.

30. Article 82: Readjustment after each census - Constitution of India.

31. *Election Commission,* Delimitation | Election Commission of India (eci.gov.in) accessed on 18/07/2024.

32. *India Code,* a1951-43.pdf (indiacode.nic.in).

33. Various Amendments of Representation of Peoples Acts - GKToday.

34. For Model Code of Conduct, see Model Code of Conduct | Election Commission of India (eci.gov.in) ; for EVM and VVPAT, see History of EVM - Election Commission of India (eci.gov.in); for SVEEP, see About Us - Systematic Voters' Education and Electoral Participation (ecisveep.nic.in).

Appendix

A

A Note on Amendments Curtailing the Scope of Fundamental Rights

Fundamental Rights have been amended several times since 1951. Most amendments in post-1978 period have tended to enlarge the scope of a certain Right. Thus, the Seventy-Seventh, Ninety-Third and One Hundred and Third Amendments have expanded the scope of affirmative action by including new sections of people under the policy of Reservation. The Eighty-Sixth Amendment has inserted Article 21A, resulting in Right to Education becoming a Fundamental Right.[1] On the other hand, amendments prior to 1978 tended to restrict the scope of Fundamental Rights. These are discussed in brief below.

FIRST AMENDMENT, 1951

Three different factors contributed to the making of the First Amendment. One of them was a series of decisions by various HCs—either striking down laws seeking to abolish zamindari; and/or accepting the petitions for fair compensation for acquired properties. Second factor was verdicts of the courts upholding the freedom of speech and expression against the censorship attempts of the Government. And the third factor was the ruling of the HCs, specifically the Madras HC, striking down special provisions made by the State government in college admissions for the backward classes.[2]

The First Amendment was passed on 10 June 1951 by the CA in its capacity as the interim Parliament. It was an extensive amendment, and resulted in amending many Articles in Part III.[3] Firstly, the Amendment attempted to protect the zamindari abolition programme of the Government vis-à-vis the Right to Property of individuals.

Thus, it inserted Article 31A, protecting laws abolishing Zamindari from judicial intervention, even if they encroached upon certain other fundamental rights. It further inserted Article 31B which created the Ninth Schedule, providing that any law included in the Ninth Schedule will not be subject to judicial review.

Secondly, introduced more severe restrictions on Article 19(1)(a). Thus, it replaced Article 19(2) with an entirely new clause. The list of restrictions on the Freedom of Speech and Expression was already very long in the 1950 Constitution—libel, slander, defamation, contempt of court, decency or morality, security of the state. The amended version of the Clause added more restrictions, viz. friendly relations with foreign States, public order, and incitement to an offence. The Amendment made an already weak Freedom of Expression extremely feeble, if not non-existent.

Thirdly, the Amendment added clause 15(4) to the Right to Equality. This extended the power of the State to make special provisions to the socially and educationally backward classes and the Scheduled Castes and Scheduled Tribes.

The bill was condemned by the press and was fiercely debated in the Interim Parliament. President Rajendra Prasad had expressed his opposition to the proposed amendment before the draft was finalised. Speaker G.V. Mavlankar expressed his objections to the bill before it was introduced in the house. Congressmen like H.V. Kamath, Deshbandhu Gupta, opposition members like S.P. Mookerjee of Hindu Mahasabha and independent member H.N. Kunzru were among the many who offered scathing criticism through very convincing arguments against the bill, tearing into the Government's position, during the debate in the house. Despite this, the Amendment was passed by required majority in the house. The most significant, and disturbing, feature of the First Amendment was that it was passed *before* the first General Election was conducted; and thus, *before* even the full bicameral parliament was formed. It was passed by the CA in its capacity as the Interim Parliament.

Perhaps the worst outcome of the Amendment was the assault on a core individual freedom, of Speech and Expression. It may not be an exaggeration to say that, if one thinks that the Freedom of Speech and Expression is nearly absent in India, then the root cause for the same is the Constitution as adopted in 1950, and the First Amendment, 1951. Judiciary, having accepted the right and power of the Parliament to amend the Fundamental Rights, is left only with judging the 'reasonableness' of restrictions imposed by the law and the government from time to time. Unfortunately, the controversy over the First Amendment ended quickly and was put to rest after the SC upheld the Amendment in Shankari Prasad judgement, 1951.

FOURTH AMENDMENT, 1955

Three court judgements in 1953 led the Nehru government to introduce another amendment, the Fourth Amendment.[4] In the first of these cases, the SC upheld the Calcutta HC decision in Bela Banerjee case which laid down that "compensation" has to be 'just' equivalent of deprived property. In the second case—S.G. Bose case—the SC asserted the authority of the court to ascertain the rightness of compensation. The third case, Sholapur Mills case, decided that compensation must be given to the shareholder, even if the Mill was not "bought", and the Government had only overtaken the management. Irked by these verdicts, the Government and the Party decided to amend the Constitution. The Fourth Amendment was passed in April 1955.[5] It amended Article 31(2) and inserted in it a provision that saved all laws providing compensation for acquired property from judicial review. It also amended Article 31A, protecting laws acquiring property from being declared void on the ground of violating the Rights in Articles 14, 19 and 31. It further expanded the Ninth Schedule.

SIXTEENTH AMENDMENT, 1963

The Sixteenth Amendment inserted the words "sovereignty and integrity of India" to Article 19(2), the list of restrictions on Freedom of Speech and Expression. It also added these words to Article 19(3), thus, adding to restrictions on the Right to Assemble peaceably and without arms. Further, this Amendment added the words to the Forms of Oaths or Affirmations in the Third Schedule.[6] Granville Austin argues, that the inclusion of these words to Article 19 was caused by the Chinese aggression; while inclusion in the Third Schedule was caused by the movement for the Punjabi Suba and the demand for an independent nation-state of Dravida Nadu.[7] Thus, the Amendment resulted in more restrictions on the Freedom of Speech and Expression.

SEVENTEENTH AMENDMENT

The SC ruled in Purushothaman case, 1961 that the word 'estate' in Article 31A did not apply to the land taken by the government from the aggrieved party, and therefore, the acquisition is not protected from judicial review.[8] This verdict is the cause behind the passing of the Seventeenth Amendment, 1964. It added Clause (2) to Article 31A. This Clause expanded the definition of the word 'estate' to include all versions of property known locally by different names. It effectively kept all laws (Union and State) made to acquire property beyond the power of judicial review on the grounds of violation of Rights under Article 14 and 19.

TWENTY-FOURTH AND TWENTY-FIFTH AMENDMENTS

Events since 1968 formed the background of the Twenty-Fourth and Twenty-Fifth Amendments. Significant of them were nationalisation of fourteen major banks (July 1969) and abolition of Privy Purses (September 1970).[9] The Indira Gandhi Government issued an ordinance to nationalise banks, just days before the Parliament convened. It was later converted into an Act. The ordinance was challenged in the SC and was struck down in February 1970. The bill to abolish Privy Purses failed to secure the required 2/3 majority in Rajya Sabha, and thus, could not be passed. The Indira Gandhi Government then resorted to issuing a Presidential order, derecognising the Princes. The order was challenged by Madhavrao Scindia, the former ruler of Gwalior, in the court. The SC decision in December 1970 declared the order as null and void.

The reaction of Indira Gandhi was similar to that of Nehru earlier—amend the Constitution when the SC strikes down the 'social agenda' of the Government. However, Indira Gandhi did not have the required 2/3 majority in the Parliament in 1970. After the mid-term elections in 1971, her party returned to power with the required majority. Mrs. Gandhi's government passed two amendments in 1971.

The Twenty-fourth Amendment added Clause (4) to Article 13, explicitly allowing the Parliament to make an amendment under Article 368 to make changes in the Rights. It changed the title of Article 368 as "Power of Parliament to Amend the Constitution and Procedure Therefor", thus, nullifying the objection of the Golaknath judgement.[10] The Twenty-fifth Amendment substituted Article 31(2) with a new Clause which said that, laws determining compensation for acquired property will not be challenged in any court on the ground of inadequate compensation. It also inserted Article 31C, saving laws giving effect to provisions of Article 39 of Directive Principles from judicial review.[11]

FORTY-SECOND AMENDMENT, 1976

During the Emergency, the Indira Gandhi Government sought to change the fundamental principles of Indian Constitution through an amendment, i.e. the Forty-Second Amendment.[12] The introduction of the Amendment in the Parliament was preceded by calls from various levels of the ruling party, for calling a new constituent assembly, writing a new constitution, converting the Parliament into a constituent assembly, and so on. It was argued that a fundamental change was required because there were many hurdles to achieving the 'socialistic pattern of society'.

The proposed Amendment met with criticism both outside and within the Parliament. Criticism outside was far more vocal. Due to the arrests of leaders under Emergency, the opposition in the Parliament was quite weak. P.G. Mavalankar (an Independent member) and Krishna Kant (a Congressman, who later became the Vice President) opposed the Amendment. But it was passed, predictably, with big majority in both Houses.

The Amendment was quite extensive in scope.[13] Only those aspects of the Amendment that affected the Fundamental Rights are noted here. It extended the scope of Article 31C; and protected all laws giving effect to any Directive Principle from judicial review, even if they encroached upon any Fundamental Right. Further, the Amendment inserted Clauses (4) and (5) in Article 368, effectively making Parliament's power to amend the Constitution unlimited, and beyond challenge in the court. The judgement in the Minerva Mills case, 1980, struck down Articles 368(4) and 368(5) and the changes made to Article 31C, as unconstitutional.[14]

FORTY-FOURTH AMENDMENT, 1978

After winning the post-Emergency election in 1977, the Janata Party Government led by Prime Minister Morarji Desai initiated a process of undoing the damage done to the Constitution by the Forty-Second Amendment. Thus, it introduced the Forty-fourth Amendment.[15] A lot of consultation and discussion had preceded the actual amendment bill.[16] Retired Justices H.R. Khanna and P.B. Gajendragadkar were among those consulted by the Government. The Amendment passed the Lok Sabha, but encountered difficulties in the Rajya Sabha, as the Janata Party did not have the required 2/3 majority in that House. Important provisions that failed to pass in the Rajya Sabha were amendments to Articles 31C and 368. It was the first time a bill passed by Lok Sabha had been changed and returned by the Rajya Sabha. The Lok Sabha, after a lengthy discussion, accepted the changes and the Amendment was, thus, passed.

The single most important change the Forty-Fourth Amendment made to Fundamental Rights was the deletion of Article 31. Section 6 of this Amendment deleted the already severely curtailed Article 31. The Right to Property was no more a Fundamental Right. A modified version of Article 31 was inserted as Article 300A.[17] This retained the Right to Property as a legal right.

ENDNOTES

1. See 77th Amendment, The Constitution (Seventy-seventh Amendment) Act, 1995| National Portal of India ; 93rd Amendment, THE CONSTITUTION (NINETY-THIRD AMENDMENT) ACT, 2005 ; 103rd Amendment 3228GI. p65; 86th Amendment, The Constitution (Eighty-sixth Amendment) Act, 2002| National Portal of India.
2. Granville Austin (1999), *Working a Democratic Constitution,* (OUP, 1999), pp ; see also Tripur Daman Singh *Sixteen Stormy Days: The Story of the First Amendment to the Constitution of India* (Vintage Books, 2020), which is a recent and an extensive historical study of the making of the First Amendment.
3. See THE CONSTITUTION (FIRST AMENDMENT) ACT, 1951| National Portal of India.
4. Austin (1999), *op cit,* p 100.
5. The Constitution (Fourth Amendment) Act, 1955| National Portal of India.
6. The Constitution (Sixteenth Amendment) Act, 1963| National Portal of India.
7. Austin (1999), *op cit,* p 51.
8. For the case, see Purushothaman Nambudiri vs The State of Kerala on 5 December, 1961 ; Austin (1999), p 111 explains how this judgement led to the Seventeenth Amendment 1964.
9. For full details of the events, see Austin (1999), *op cit,* Chapter 9.
10. The Constitution (Twenty-fourth Amendment) Act, 1971| National Portal of India.
11. The Constitution (Twenty-fifth Amendment) Act, 1971| National Portal of India.
12. For details, see Austin (1999), *op cit,* Chapters 19.
13. The Constitution (Forty-second Amendment) Act, 1976| National Portal of India.
14. See Minerva Mills vs Union of India : a significant case that India has forgotten - iPleaders.
15. The Constitution (Forty-fourth Amendment) Act, 1978| National Portal of India.
16. For details, see Austin (1999), *op cit,* Chapters 16 and 17.
17. Article 300A: Persons not to be deprived of property save by authority of law - Constitution of India.

Appendix

B

A Note on Major Supreme Court Decisions

BRIJ BHUSHAN VS STATE OF DELHI, 1950[1]

The official publication of the Rashtriya Swayamsevak Sangh (RSS), *The Organiser* was served with an order of pre-censorship by the Delhi Government, for criticising the policies of Nehru Government regarding refugees and relations with Pakistan. Brij Bhushan, the publisher of the weekly, went to SC to get the order quashed. The SC ruled that freedom of speech and expression can be restricted only on grounds mentioned in Article 19(2), and public order is not one of them. Thus, the SC declared the censorship order as illegal.

ROMESH THAPPAR VS STATE OF MADRAS, 1950[2]

Romesh Thappar was a journalist and a Marxist, with the publication called *Crossroads*. The Madras State banned the publication of Crossroads. Thappar went to the SC against the order. The SC invalidated the law of Madras State under which the publication was banned.

STATE OF MADRAS VS CHAMPAKAM DORAIRAJAN, 1951[3]

In this case, an order of the Madras State Government, called the Communal G.O. was challenged. The Communal General Order (G.O.) allotted quota of seats to Non-Brahmins, Backward Hindus, Brahmins, Harijans, Anglo-Indians and Muslims, in admission to engineering and medical colleges. The order was invalidated by the SC on grounds that it contravened Articles 29(2) and 14.

(**Note:** The above rulings, as well as the ruling by the Patna HC declaring the Bihar Land Reforms Act invalid; together caused the First Amendment to the Constitution.)

A.K. GOPALAN VS STATE OF MADRAS, 1950[4]

A.K. Gopalan, a Communist leader in the State of Madras was detained, first under criminal laws and then under the Preventive Detention Act (PDA). He filed a writ of Habeas Corpus against the order of detention in the SC. The SC held that the PDA does not contravene the Constitution, and upheld the law. It further ruled that courts can invalidate a law only if the procedure as established by the Constitution and law is not followed. Thus, it emphasised that the Constitution has accepted the principle of "procedure established by law", and not the principle of "due process". (It may be noted that B.R. Ambedkar had explained the reasons for preference for the former over the latter principle, during the CA debates.)

SHANKARI PRASAD VS UNION OF INDIA, 1951[5]

Shankari Prasad Singh Deo, a Zamindar from West Bengal, and others filed a case in the SC challenging the First Amendment, 1950. In a landmark decision, the SC upheld the First Amendment. It ruled that the Provisional Parliament does have the right to amend the Constitution under Article 368. It also ruled that the word 'law' in Article 13 does not include an 'amendment'; meaning thereby, that the Fundamental Rights are amendable, and can be amended by an amendment under Article 368.

STATE OF WEST BENGAL VS BELA BANERJEE, 1954[6]

This was another case regarding land acquisition. The West Bengal Development and Planning Act, 1948 proposed to acquire land primarily for the settlement of refugees coming from East Pakistan into the State. The compensation for the acquired land was fixed at not exceeding the market value of the same as on 31 December 1946. An appeal was filed against the decisions in the lower court by the State of West Bengal. The SC ruled the said Act as ultra vires and declared it as void. It reasoned that an Act of permanent nature cannot freeze the value of compensation. Further, the SC laid down that "compensation" means a just equivalent of what the owner has been deprived of; and the principle determining the same is a justiciable issue to be adjudicated by the courts.

SAJJAN SINGH VS STATE OF RAJASTHAN, 1964[7]

This case was filed to question the validity of the Seventeenth Amendment (See Appendix I). The SC upheld the Amendment as valid. It also reiterated the position of the Shankari Prasad verdict that the Parliament has the power to amend the Constitution under Article 368.

GOLAKNATH VS STATE OF PUNJAB, 1967[8]

The Golaknath family had owned over 500 acres of land in the district of Jalandhar. A huge part of the land was declared 'surplus' by the Punjab Government under the Punjab Security and Land Tenures Act. The Act was placed in the Ninth Schedule by the Seventeenth Amendment. The Golaknath family challenged the Punjab Act as well as the Seventeenth Amendment in the court. The case was heard by a 11-judge bench of the SC and the verdict was given by a thin margin of 6:5.[9] Reversing the earlier position of the SC, the majority judgement ruled that Fundamental Rights cannot be amended by the Parliament. The word 'Law' in Article 13 *includes* an amendment. It remarked that the cases challenging the First and the Seventeenth Amendments were wrongly decided.

R.C. COOPER VS UNION BANK OF INDIA, 1970 (BANK NATIONALISATION CASE)[10]

The Indira Gandhi Government issued an ordinance to nationalise 14 major commercial banks. The ordinance was later converted into an Act by the Parliament. It was challenged in the SC by R.C. Cooper, a shareholder in one of the banks that were nationalised. The SC gave its decision by 10:1 majority.[11] It struck down the act in February 1970 on the ground that it violated Article 31 as well as Article 14.

MADHAVRAO SCINDIA VS UNION OF INDIA, 1970 (PRIVY PURSES CASE)[12]

The bill to abolish Privy Purses failed to secure the required 2/3 majority in Rajya Sabha, and thus, could not be passed. The Indira Gandhi Government then resorted to issuing a Presidential order, derecognising the Princes. The order was challenged by Madhavrao Scindia, the former ruler of Gwalior, in the court. The SC declared the order as null and void in December 1970.[13]

KESAVANANDA BHARATI VS STATE OF KERALA, 1973[14]

The Head of a Hindu monastery in Kerala, Kesavananda Bharati, filed a case against the attempts of the State Government of Kerala to impose restrictions on the management of the property of the monastery under the land reforms acts of the State. The case challenged the Acts, as well as the validity of the

Twenty-Fourth, Twenty-Fifth, Twenty-Sixth and Twenty-Ninth Amendments. The case was heard by a 13-judge bench and gave a verdict by 7:6 majority.[15]

The decision of the majority reversed the position of the Golaknath judgement. It declared that the Parliament has the power to amend the Constitution, including the Fundamental Rights. The SC upheld the four Amendments questioned in the case and declared them valid. However, the SC also held that, while the Parliament has the power to amend the Constitution, this power is not unlimited. The Parliament cannot amend what the judges called the "Basic Structure" of the Constitution. CJI Sikri explained what constitutes the Basic Structure of the Constitution, as: supremacy of the Constitution, separation of the major governmental institutions, federalism, secularism, democracy and republican nature of the Constitution. Some other judges added more features to the "Basic Structures", namely: unity and integrity of the nation, freedom of the individual, sovereignty of the nation, parliamentary democracy, egalitarian society, dignity of individual as expressed by both, the fundamental rights and the welfare state.

This is regarded as a landmark decision because of the establishment of the Doctrine of Basic Structure. This Doctrine limited the power of the Parliament to amend the Constitution on the one hand, and on the other, became a source of Judicial Review.

ADM JABALPUR VS SHIVKANT SHUKLA, 1976 (HABEAS CORPUS CASE)[16]

Many opposition leaders were arrested under the Maintenance of Internal Security Act (MISA) during Emergency. Many of the arrested leaders filed petition of Habeas Corpus in respective HCs. HCs of Delhi, Karnataka and Madhya Pradesh ordered the release of the leaders. The Government of India appealed to the SC against these verdicts. The judgement, given by a majority of 4:1, shocked most people.[17] The court held that when an order of Emergency is issued, the Fundamental Rights and their protection stand suspended. Thus, no person has any locus standi to file any writ petition in the court.

RELIGIOUS CONVERSION AND STANISLAUS CASE, 1977

The Legislative Assembly of the State of Orissa passed the Freedom of Religion Act in 1967. The law prevents conversion of a person from one religion to another by force, by inducements or by fraudulent means. In 1968, Madhya Pradesh state passed a similar law, seeking to prevent forced conversions on the same grounds. Appeals on the verdicts of the respective HCs came before the SC. The objection against the laws was that it took away the freedom in Article 25(1), to 'propagate' religion.

A five-judge bench ruled unanimously, that "what the Article grants is not the right to convert another person to one's own religion, but to transmit or spread one's religion by an exposition of its tenets." The judgement said that the Rights conferred in Articles 25 and 26 are "expressly made subject to public order, morality and health". It further said that forcible conversions could lead to raising communal passions, and it could "in all probability, give rise to an apprehension of a breach of the public order, affecting the community at large."[18] This verdict, that 'right to propagate does not mean right to conversion', has not yet been overruled. In a recent decision, the Himachal Pradesh HC struck down parts of state conversion law which imposed criminal sanctions on those converting without intimidation. However, it did uphold those provisions similar to those upheld in the Stanislaus case.[19]

Currently, six states in India have laws preventing forcible conversion. These are: Odisha (1967), Madhya Pradesh (1968), Gujarat (2003), Chhatisgarh (2006), Himachal Pradesh (2006), Jharkhand (2017).

(**Note:** There is a new wave of anti-conversion laws that began with the state of Uttarakhand passing its "Freedom of Religion" Act in 2018. It seeks to prevent conversion by force, misrepresentation, undue influence, coercion, allurement or by any fraudulent means and also by marriage. The States of Himachal Pradesh (2019), Uttar Pradesh (2020), Madhya Pradesh (2020), Karnataka (2021), Haryana (2022) have followed the trend. A bunch of petitions challenging these laws is pending in the SC.)

MANEKA GANDHI VS UNION OF INDIA, 1978[20]

Maneka Gandhi, a journalist, was asked to return her passport by the Ministry of External Affairs in July 1977. When she asked the reason for the action, it was stated as 'in the interest of general public'. Ms. Gandhi filed a petition in the SC arguing that her Fundamental Rights under Articles 14, 19 and 21 were violated by the order. This case revolved around the interpretation of the phrases 'personal liberty' and 'procedure established by law' in Article 21. The judgement overturned the interpretation of these phrases in A.K. Gopalan case, 1950, as well as the interpretation of the term 'procedure established by law'. The judgement significantly widened the meaning of the term personal liberty, and said that personal liberty includes the rights given in Article 19. It further said that the court has the power to judge not only whether personal liberty is taken away *as per the procedure of law*; but also, to judge whether that procedure is *fair and reasonable*. Thus, effectively, the judgement established the 'due process' doctrine in jurisprudence and it became the basis of judicial review.

MINERVA MILLS VS UNION OF INDIA, 1980[21]

A textile mill near Bangalore, the Minerva Mill was overtaken by the National Textile Corporation in 1971. The petitioners challenged it in the SC. The SC gave its verdict by 4:1 majority.[22] It invalidated the part of Article 31C which prevented judicial review of any law giving effect to any Directive Principle, on the grounds of violating Fundamental Rights. The verdict also declared void Clause (5) that was added to Article 368 by the Forty-Second Amendment, which prevented judicial review of any amendment made to the Constitution. This decision is a landmark in that it restored the power of judicial review, which the Parliament had attempted to curtail by Emergency era Amendment.

INDRA SAWHNEY VS UNION OF INDIA, 1992 (MANDAL COMMISSION CASE)[23]

Known by the name of its Chairman B.P. Mandal, the Mandal Commission was appointed in 1979 by the Janata Party government and submitted its report in 1980, but subsequent governments did not act upon it. Finally, Prime Minister V.P. Singh announced in August 1990 the intent of his government to implement the Report. The Mandal Commission had proposed to reserve 27% seats in educational institutions for the Other Backward Classes (OBCs). Indra Sawhney challenged this decision in the SC. In the landmark judgement delivered by 6:3 majority, the SC upheld the policy of extending reservation to the OBCs.[24] The judgement directed that reserved seats should not exceed 50% of the total seats. It also laid down the principle of "Creamy Layer", by virtue of which the advanced sections within the OBCs were excluded from reservation.

JAGADAMBIKA PAL VS UNION OF INDIA, 1998[25]

Governor of UP dismissed the government of Kalyan Singh 21 February 1998, appointed Jagadambika Pal as Chief Minister. Allahabad High Court declared the dismissal of Kalyan Singh government as unconstitutional and reinstated his government on 23 February 1998. Jagadambika Pal appealed to the SC against the Allahabad High Court decision. SC ordered a special session of UP Assembly on 26 February 1998. Vote was taken on both Singh and Pal governments, which was won by Kalyan Singh. Violence in the House was not regarded by the SC as "breakdown of Constitutional machinery".

RAMESHWAR PRASAD VS UNION OF INDIA, 2005[26]

No party secured a clear majority in the February 2005 elections to Bihar Assembly. Therefore, President's Rule was imposed on 7 March 2005. Governor informed the President of "horse trading" by parties to secure majority on 27 April 2005. President dissolved the Bihar Legislative Assembly on the advice of the Union Cabinet on 23 May 2005. The dissolution was challenged in SC. In its judgement given on 24 January 2006, the SC, by a 3:2 majority, held the dissolution of Bihar Assembly as unconstitutional. The Governor had not explored all options before recommending dissolution.

NABAM REBIA VS DEPUTY SPEAKER, 2011[27]

Nabam Tuki was Chief Minister of Arunachal Pradesh since the Congress won the State Assembly election in 2011. There were defections in the Congress in April 2014, and the rebels joined hands with BJP MLAs to attempt to form government. The Governor ordered floor test in December 2014. The Congress Speaker locked the Assembly House. The Deputy Speaker elected by rebels held the session in another building and the rebels won the floor test. The Governor decided to dismiss the Tuki government. SC declared unconstitutional all decisions of the Governor in this respect and restored the Tuki government.

UNION OF INDIA VS H.S. RAWAT, 2016[28]

Defections made the Congress government of Uttarakhand led by H.S. Rawat unstable in March 2016. Governor gave time for floor test. However, before the test, the President issued proclamation under Article 356, dismissing the Rawat government, on the grounds that Union government had obtained a CD showing Rawat distributing money. SC ordered floor test on 10 May, which was won by Rawat. His government was reinstated.

SHYRA BANO VS UNION OF INDIA, 2017 (TRIPLE TALAQ CASE)[29]

Syra Bano was divorced by her husband through instantaneous 'triple talaq' in October 2015. She file a writ petition in the SC against the practice of triple talaq claiming that it violates the Right to Equality, Right against Discrimination and the Right to Livelihood. The SC ruled by 3:2 majority that the practice of triple talaq was manifestly arbitrary and unconstitutional.[30] The minority opinion ruled the practice as protected under the freedom of religion. They also said that in this case, it is the job of the Parliament to make law in this respect.

(**Note:** In July 2019 the Parliament passed the Muslim Women Protection of Rights on Marriage Act. Triple talaq was made a punishable offence, with a possible punishment of three years imprisonment. A petition challenging the Act is filed in the SC.

INDIAN YOUNG LAWYERS ASSN. VS STATE OF KERALA, 2018 (SABARIMALA CASE)[31]

The Travancore Dewasom Board manages an Ayyappa temple located at Sabarimala, Kerala. Entry of women in menstruating age (10-50 years) is prevented in this temple, as per the tradition as well as by the Kerala Hindu Places of Public Worship Rules 1965). Indian Young Women Lawyers Association filed a case against this practice. The practice was upheld by the Kerala HC, following which the petitioners appealed to the SC. The SC gave a decision by 4:1 majority.[32] The judgement said that the practice violates Fundamental Rights to equality, liberty and freedom of religion. Stating that devotion cannot be subjected to gender discrimination, the SC allowed entry of women of all groups in the Sabarimala temple.

The minority opinion in this judgement—of Justice Indu Malhotra, who incidentally was the only woman judge on the panel—is worth a mention. Justice Malhotra upheld that the status of Ayyappa devotees is that of a separate religious denomination, and that the practice of denying entry to women in a certain age group as essential practice of the religious denomination. She said further, that secular polity and pluralistic society would ensure that the followers and believers of various sects have the freedom to practise and profess their faith adhering with the tenets of their religion.

STATE OF PUNJAB VS DAVINDER SINGH, 2024[33]

The case involved the Punjab Scheduled Caste and Backward Classes (Reservation in Services Act), 2006. The Punjab & Haryana HC struck it down in 2010. The Punjab Government appealed to the SC. The SC upheld the law by 6:1 majority.[34] It ruled that sub-categorization of SCs and STs for reservation is constitutionally valid. It said that the purpose of reservation is to uplift the most disadvantaged, and sub-categorization ensures equitable distribution of benefits.

TAMIL NADU GOVERNMENT VS TAMIL NADU GOVERNOR, 2025[35]

The Government of Tamil Nadu had filed a case in the SC against its own Governor, R.N. Ravi. The Governor had delayed assent to the bills passed by the State Legislative Assembly. A bench of Justices Pardiwala and Mahadevan ruled that the Governor cannot reserve the bill for consideration of the President after the Legislative Assembly has reconsidered and passed it second time. In such condition, it is mandatory for the Governor to give his assent. The SC said that the Governor cannot delay the assent to a bill indefinitely. It laid down a time-line under Article 200 for giving assent. The SC also ruled that even the President cannot withhold assent indefinitely to a bill sent by a Governor for his consideration. A delay in giving assent by President is also open to judicial scrutiny.

ENDNOTES

1. Arun Anand "Nehru vs RSS-backed Organiser" *The Print,* 07 June 2021 Nehru vs RSS-backed Organiser: A battle that led to curbs on our freedom of expression.
2. Romesh Thappar vs The State of Madras on 26 May, 1950.
3. The State of Madras vs Srimathi Champakam Dorairajan and the ... on 9 April, 1951.
4. AK Gopalan vs State of Madras (1950) - iPleaders.
5. Shankari Prasad Case [Shankari Prasad vs Union of India].
6. The State of West Bengal vs Mrs. Bela Banerjee and Others on 11 December, 1953.
7. Sajjan Singh vs State of Rajasthan (With Connected ... on 30 October, 1964.
8. I. C. Golaknath & Ors vs State of Punjab & Anrs. (With Connected ... on 27 February, 1967.)
9. The majority was formed by CJI Subba Rao, and Justices J.C. Shah, S.M. Sikri, J.M. Shelat, C.A. Vaidiyalingam, with Justice Hidayatullah concurring and the minority was formed by Justices K.N. Wanchoo, V. Bhargav, G.K. Mitter, R.S. Bachawat and V. Ramaswami.
10. R.C. Cooper vs Union of India: bank nationalisation case summary - iPleaders.
11. Justices Shah, Sikri, Shelat, Bhargava, Mitter, Vaidialingam, Hegde, Grover, Reddy and Dua formed the majority. Justice Ray was the only dissenting judge.
12. MADHAV JIWAJI RAO SCINDIA V. UNION OF INDIA 1970 - The Legal Lock.
13. The majority comprised CJI Hidayatullah, Justices Shah, Vaidialingam, Hegde, Grover and Dua. Justices Mitter and Ray dissented.
14. Kesavananda Bharati vs State of Kerala (1973): case analysis.
15. There were 11 separate judgements, with agreement of certain issues and disagreement on others. The majority consisted of CJI Sikri, Justices Hegde, Mukherjea, Shelat, Grover, Reddy, Khanna. The minority comprised Justices A.N. Ray, Palekar, Mathew, Beg, Dwivedi, Chandrachud.
16. Additional District Magistrate, ... vs S. S. Shukla on 28 April, 1976.
17. The majority comprised CJI Ray, Justices Beg, Chandrachud and Bhagwati. Justice Khanna was the lone dissenter.
18. Rev. Stainislaus vs State of Madhya Pradesh & Ors on 17 January, 1977 (indiankanoon.org) The five judges were A.N. Ray, M.H. Beg, R.S. Sarkaria, P.N. Shingal and Jaswant Singh.
19. Alok Prasanna Kumar "Myth and Rhetoric: Dissecting the anti-conversion law" *Deccan Herald* 19 December 2021, Myth and rhetoric: Dissecting the anti-conversion law (deccanherald.com).

20. Maneka Gandhi vs Union of India, 1978 AIR 597 1978 SCR (2) 621 197.
21. Minerva Mills vs Union of India: A significant case that India has forgotten - iPleaders.
22. Justice Bhagwati was the lone dissenter, whereas CJI Chandrachud, Justices Gupta, Untwalia and Kailasam formed the majority opinion.
23. Indra Sawhney vs Union of India and Ors. (1992): case analysis (ipleaders.in).
24. CJI M.H. Kania, Justices M.N. Venkatachaliah, S.R. Pandian, A.M. Ahmadi, P.B. Sawant and B.P. Jeevan Reddy formed the majority opinion, whereas Justices T.K. Thommen, Kuldip Singh and R.M. Sahai formed the minority opinion.
25. In 1998 UP case, SC had ordered composite floor test to end row | India News - Times of India.
26. https://legalvidhiya.com/rameshwar-prasad-v-union-of-india-air-2006-sc-980/.
27. President's Rule: Judgment Summary - Supreme Court Observer.
28. https://www.jlsrjournal.in/case-commentary-on-harish-chandra-singh-rawat-v-union-of-india-by-archana-goswami/.
29. Triple Talaq - Supreme Court Observer.
    https://www.scobserver.in/cases/shayara-bano-union-india-triple-talaq-case-background/.
30. Justices Kurian Joseph, R.F. Nariman and U.U. Lalit formed the majority while the CJI Khehar and Justice Abdul Nazeer gave the minority opinion.
31. The Sabrimala Verdict: A Complete Analysis and also see Indian Young Lawyers Association & Ors. vs The State of Kerala & Ors. (2018).
32. CJI Deepak Mishra, Justices A.N. Khanwilkar, Rohintan Nariman and D.Y. Chandrachud formed the majority opinion whereas Justice Indu Malhotra formed the minority opinion.
33. Landmark Supreme Court Verdict on SC/ST Quota: Sub-Categorization Allowed | State of Punjab vs Davinder Singh (2024), see also Validity of Sub-Classification Within Reserved Categories - Supreme Court Observer.
34. The majority comprised CJI Chandrachud, Justices Gavai, Nath, Mithal, Misra, Sharma, while Justice Bela Trivedi gave the dissenting opinion.
35. EXPLAINER | Supreme Court landmark ruling on Governor vs State.

Index